Chester L Schwartz

Apr. — 1928.

Indianapolis Area
A Record and History

CHRIST FIRST

The Indianapolis Area

OF

The Methodist Episcopal Church

1924-1928

A Record and History

CLARENCE E. FLYNN, *Editor*

PUBLISHED BY THE AREA COUNCIL
INDIANAPOLIS

PREVIOUS VOLUME

The Indianapolis Area of the Methodist Episcopal Church

1920-1924

PRINTED BY
HERALD PUBLISHING COMPANY
ANDERSON, INDIANA

PUBLICATION COMMITTEE

For This Volume

C. E. FLYNN, Chairman.   W. B. FARMER, Secretary.

The bishop, district superintendents, and conference secretaries of the Area, members ex officio.

G. O. Carpenter

H. L. Davis	C. C. Hall	F. A. Hall
C. O. Holmes	J. W. McFall	J. M. Mitchell
J. A. Rowe	A. H. Sapp	W. G. Seaman

T. F. Williams

List *of* Illustrations

᷒

Table *of* Contents

᪥

I. INTRODUCTION

II. THE AREA   *Page*

III. THE CONFERENCES

IV. THE DISTRICTS

CONTENTS—Continued

∾

CONTENTS—Continued

❧

Introduction

THE present volume is an attempt to visualize and suggest in a concrete but highly general way the life and work of the Indianapolis Area during the second quadrennium of its existence cast against the background of its past. These pages will bring interesting information to those who read them now. Should they be preserved during the life of one or more generations they will have for those who read them in the future an interest increasing in direct proportion to the time that will have elapsed. It is therefore a service to the present, but it is even more a service to the future which is here attempted.

This volume is published with the idea that the history of a church is important, even as is the history of a nation. Too little effort has been made to preserve the shrines and records of Methodist history. The result is that hallowed spots have fallen into neglect, and in some instances have even been lost altogether, while the story of many a brave exploit, memorable service, and remarkable experience has remained unrecorded, or has been lost among the drifts of time. This volume is the expression of our desire that it shall not be entirely so with this particular period.

The Indianapolis Area is new. It has known only one episcopal administration, but during the brief period of its existence it has given good account of itself. This is the second of two quadrennial volumes to have recorded a portion of its progress. Less than a decade ago this Area was an idea. Today it is one of the most compactly and effectively organized areas in the connection. Its scope is so broad and its labors so abundant that many more pages than this would be required even to suggest them adequately.

The purpose of the committee issuing this book has been, not to publish a highly ornamental volume, but rather to make a plain and practical collection of important information. It is intended to be a book for the library, and our hope is that its usefulness will be more or less permanent.

The present volume only reflects a few of the high lights of the Indianapolis Area. Most futile would be the attempt to make any single book really representative of a life so deep, of a hope so large, and of activities so many and varied. This is a picture of broad outlines. No attempt can be made to sketch in the detail. Yet the detail exists, and it is important. Almost any day of the history of Methodism in the Indianapolis Area would make a book, while this book must cover the passage of many days.

A few churches, a few institutions, and a few individuals are mentioned here, but they are only taken as representative of the larger number of churches and the greater multitude of people making up the Area as a whole. We are not unmindful of the humblest maker of the briefest prayer, the smallest gift of the youngest child, and the necessary undergirding of the life of the Kingdom that comes from the faith and the service of the great host of nameless Christian men and women in the background of the picture. It is really a story of their sacrifices and labors, of their love and faith, and the largest honors it has to suggest are for them.

Although in detail the Indianapolis Area organization is the work of many hands and many minds, in general it has sprung from the heart and brain of one man, the resident Bishop. The last to be willing to admit it, Bishop Frederick DeLand Leete, has really made this Area what it is, and therefore has truly made this book possible. Seldom are such pieces of organization brought into existence so effectively in so short a time. Only genius can do it, and genius has been at the helm here during the eight year period now closing.

My personal thanks are hereby extended to the Area Publication Committee, the cooperation of the members of which has been willing and complete, to the various individuals who have so readily consented to contribute sections and who have so well prepared the material included, and to all who in any way, known or unknown, have contributed to the making of this book.

We have tried to make this a book of the Kingdom. It deals with the affairs of only one church organization, but Methodism claims only her own place among the many branches of the Church Universal, and carries on her work as the contribution of one Christian body to the united program of Christendom. It deals with facts, and figures, and organizations, and titles, but it does so only in the effort to set forth the fact that out of the poor efforts of human hands, the material existence of the human institutions, and the inadequate functioning of human organizations rises day by day the spiritual beauty of the Kingdom of God.

Clarence E. Flynn.

The Area

....

A WORD FROM THE AREA BISHOP

AT THE earnest request of the editor of this volume, whose good work and that of those cooperating with him have put us all in debt, I am penning for this page a few lines of sincere good-will.

Not farewell, but fare thee well, is my message. Within a few days the sphere of whatever labors God may assign to me will be somewhere other than in Indiana and Illinois. Wherever Mrs. Leete and I may reside we will still have very great interest in the undertakings and successes of Methodism hereabouts.

When I move, I move—physically, but not spiritually. Deeply concerned as I am for the progress of the Kingdom of Christ in all regions, I have a peculiar and I think natural ambition for the increasing success of Christian undertakings in those places where my own ministry has been spent. It will be my prayer that your future achievements may far exceed those which have characterized the past eight years of history of the Indianapolis Area.

Fare thee well, beloved—in basket and store, in health and happiness, but above all else in Christian experience and activity! One thing is most worth while—the love and service of God. "Godliness is profitable unto all things: having promise of the life which now is and of that which is to come."

Your fellow-laborer in Christ,

FREDERICK D. LEETE.

AREA FACTS

This Area has the second largest membership in the Methodist Episcopal Church; 7,252 preparatory members, 28,295 non-resident, 337,944 in full membership; grand total, 373,491.

This is the only Area in the American Church which has gained in membership each of the past eight years. In net increases we have been among the first four areas every year, having been first once, third four times and fourth three times.

56,946 net gain in members is the record of the eight years' life of Indianapolis Area. Our adopted goal was 50,000. Under the divine blessing, we have more than attained the objective.

This Area has 4 conferences, 22 districts with 1,346 preachers, all included. We have 1,853 churches and 1,033 parsonages with a total recorded valuation of $28,402,141.

Our Sunday schools have a total enrollment of 326,010 members with an excellent proportional average attendance. 41,000 young people are in Senior and Junior Epworth Leagues.

All organizations of Christian women recognized by our Church are represented strongly in the Area, as shown elsewhere in this volume. The total giving of these societies is large and increasing.

Twenty institutions represent Area activities. We have 4 colleges and universities, 2 Wesley Foundations, 4 Epworth League institutes, one girls' school, 5 hospitals, 2 homes for the aged, 2 orphanages. Their assets are around eleven millions of dollars.

The Methodist Hospital of Indianapolis is one of the two largest in the connection. This year 200 new beds with a future plan for 200 more will make this institution easily first in size and in efficiency.

Financial gains, as recorded elsewhere in this book, have kept pace with the spiritual progress of this Area. Our Area motto and constant emphasis has been "Christ First." The ideal is high, and we come far short of it, but it is in our thought and purpose.

Our Area Leader

Bishop Frederick D. Leete

SECOND QUADRENNIAL REPORT

INDIANAPOLIS AREA, METHODIST EPISCOPAL CHURCH.

Frederick D. Leete, Resident Bishop.

This is the official report as presented to the General Conference held at Kansas City, Missouri, May, 1928, and covering the years 1924-1928.

The four conferences of Indianapolis Area cover the state of Indiana except for colored and language churches, together with that part of the state of Illinois south of the Vandalia railroad. There are twenty-two districts in this territory.

Membership Gain 24,125

Conference net gains for the last four years as gathered from the published minutes are shown in the following table:

Indiana	10,178
North Indiana	3,543
Northwest Indiana	5,421
Southern Illinois	4,983
Total net gain	24,125

These figures include a small gain in probationers now on the roll, 485, an increase of 8,587 in the non-resident column and an addition to full membership lists of 15,053. The area has made net gains each of the four years of the quadrennium and each conference, save one, has shown an increase every year.

Over 50,000 *Added Members in Eight Years.*

One of the goals adopted when the area began its planning eight years since was an increase of 50,000 members in the period which has now been covered. The earnest pastors and members of our conference took this objective seriously. There have been no evangelistic conventions, nor has any pressure been exerted other than that of Christian idealism and expectancy. A strong, believing and purposeful gospel has been preached in the pulpits of the area with few exceptions. All proper methods of evangelistic effort have been employed in various parts of the field. The outcome is a net increase every one of the eight years since the organization of this area, and a total gain in membership for the two quadrenniums of 56,946.

The present membership of Indianapolis Area is as follows:

	Preparatory	Full Membership	Non-Resident
Indiana	2,304	116,822	10,208
North Indiana	2,663	94,801	5,233
Northwest Indiana	964	66,340	7,542
Southern Illinois	1,321	59,981	5,312
	7,252	337,944	28,295

Grand Total 373,491

Sixty Thousand Baptisms

It is a very satisfactory indication of Christian vitality that during the past quadrennium parents have presented for baptism 26,673 children. The adults who have received the rite of Christian baptism are 36,420. Adding the two figures we find the baptisms running to 63,093, a gratifying sum.

While it is doubtless true that a much greater ingathering might have occurred had more ardent endeavor been made by all units in this field, the above facts are certainly sufficient to prove that hereabouts are many sincere, effective Christian laborers, and that the heart of the church is spiritual.

Four and a Half Million Benevolences.

The giving of the area during the quadrennium to the various Methodist benevolences has not been as we would like. Nevertheless it is something that for all these causes, disciplinary and annual conference in character, more than a million dollars a year have been placed upon the altar. The record shows Indiana Conference, $1,472,314; North Indiana, $1,623,636; Northwest Indiana, $898,520; Southern Illinois, $506,771. The total of these figures is $4,501,241. Among the factors which prevented advances in this direction are the clear understanding of many that they were not to be called upon to maintain Centenary levels of giving, and the unquestionable need of rebuilding old and obsolete church plants and long-needed new structures deferred for years by Centenary claims. Another item has been the demands of our educational and philanthropic institutions for funds not covered in benevolent budgets. Increased pastoral support has also been asked for and obtained.

Growing Institutions.

Of the four Methodist colleges in this area, one, DePauw, has received large additional funds mainly from the estate of Edward Rector. During the quadrennium two new dormitories have been erected and $50,000 expended on the heating plant. Music Hall has received $30,000 of improvement. The increase in plant value is $586,072 and in endowment $1,624,673. Evansville College plans a campaign for additional funds. McKendree College, Lebanon, Illinois, approaches its centenary and has stabilized its finances, receiving high collegiate recognition. Taylor University, Upland, Indiana, has qualified for Indiana A grade rating, and has strengthened its financial and structural equipment. A half million dollar fund was recently completed, and another similar sum is being solicited.

Our hospitals are five, at Carbondale, Ill.; Indianapolis, Fort Wayne, Gary and Princeton, Indiana. Gary has a large new nurses' home. Indianapolis has erected a new heating-plant and laundry and a great home and school for nurses, and will at once proceed with a new hospital unit, doubling its operating facilities and enlarging its bed capacity to 585 from 385, and providing for a later increase of stories bringing the beds to 785.

The two orphanages of this area are at Mt. Vernon, Ill., and Lebanon, Indiana. The former institution has increased its property values by $54,000 and the latter has a splendid new location and buildings valued at $100,000 with a reasonable temporary debt. The Monett school for girls at Rensselaer, Indiana, continues its good and economical work.

Two homes for the aged, Lawrenceville, Illinois, and Warren, Indiana, have added new buildings, increasing their resources by over $100,000.

The combined properties and financial resources of the institutions above named are worth, less debts, in the vicinity of ten million dollars, a gain of over thirty per cent.

Two other organizations are without much property, but are exceedingly important—the Wesley Foundations at Indiana and Purdue Universities. In these state schools Methodist families are represented by about one-third of all the students enrolled. The service being rendered at Bloomington and West Lafayette is both intelligently and spiritually directed. It is a credit to the denomination and a constant reinforcement of Christian influence. Steps have been taken toward the establishment of foundations at the state normal schools in Muncie and Terre Haute.

A Church Building Period.

A few years since the Indianapolis Area was largely without architecturally attractive and adequate church plants. The desire of our people to render a more efficient service, the pressure of competition from other denominations, the increase of institutions seeking to monopolize the time and thought of church members, and the demands made by the young life of the church required the initiation of a resolute building program. The result has been the construction of a great number of large, beautiful and usable homes of Christian activity. Every portion of our territory has shared in this undertaking. Only a few cases of serious extravagance seem to have occurred, and careful computations show that current expenses have not increased in any such proportion as might be expected. Indeed the overhead cost of running our churches has decreased in one conference, has remained stationary in another, and has made normal advances in the two remaining groups. In a few districts debts are somewhat burdensome, but real embarrassments are not numerous. After deducting the existing debts our net gain in the value of our 1853 churches is $4,893,424 and the increased worth of 1,033 parsonages is $478,843, a total church property advance for the quadrennium of $5,372,267.

Vigorous Societies.

Our Sunday schools enroll 326,010 members, with an average attendance of 174,875. Epworth and Junior Leagues number more than 41,000 constituents and we have four really remarkable Epworth League institutes, including the largest in the denomination. Three of these institutes have very valuable assembly properties. A very slight decrease in some of the above enrollments may be accounted for by stricter bookkeeping or by inaccuracy in reporting.

The societies of women in the Indianapolis Area continue their steady, proportional gains in numbers and in financial results. The Ladies Aid, Calendar Club and other bodies of local workers are devoted, unselfish and reliable. The Woman's Foreign and Home Missionary Societies are models of intelligent study, stimulating administration and economic sagacity.

Preachers Aid Societies in each of the conferences of the area have done effective service, and the resources of these organizations amount to $1,810,051, a gain of $385,895 in four years.

Our chief cities have now some form of city council or union, well organized and active, for the planting of new church societies, the care of missions and the sustenance of necessary work in difficult neighborhoods. Several strong churches have resulted from the use of methods which promise continuous future developments.

The Area and the Methodism of Indiana have councils, meeting semi-annually, and operating through committees in affairs religious, philanthropic, educational and civic. The Indiana State Council is an incorporated body which has had eight years of successful life. It has made helpful decisions for its constituency, has aided many general movements, including those of evangelistic and reformatory value, and possesses funds and real property. This Council of nearly two hundred members elected by the district conferences voted at its last meeting to become permanent.

The Indianapolis Area furnishes more than 15,000 subscribers to the Western Christian Advocate, helping to make it the Methodist paper whose income exceeds expenses. Increases of pastoral support in the four conferences have ranged from ten to thirty-two per cent.

Concluding Items.

My own personal effort has been devoted to thinking, planning and co-operating, insofar as these processes might be likely to advance the interests of this portion of the Kingdom. It has been a constant care to seek improvement of pastoral personnel, and this has been measurably accomplished. Cases of moral obliquity have been as exceedingly few as conference discipline has been impartial and prompt. The superintendents and pastoral forces of the area can be compared creditably with those of any portion of the church. I desire to express my appreciation of all that has been done by our disinterested devoted preachers and of the generous co-operation and consideration of the men and women of the laity.

It is a pleasure to be able to report that there are no apparent cleavages or hostilities between our forces. There are no general enterprises which I have initiated or for which I have signed any obligation by which my successor will be embarrassed.

In closing my fourth quadrennial report it is a personal satisfaction to me to know that whatever of value or demerit may attach to my pastoral career and my sixteen years of episcopal labor, the work has not been financially costly to the Church. It would be possible for me to show that the entire sum of my ministerial salaries and expenses for forty years of labor have been more than met in each of two ways, in sums which during this time I have secured for Methodist undertakings from sources outside the denomination, and in increased values of properties which I have purchased personally or through agents for religious uses. My debt of gratitude to the Church—an exceedingly deep one—is of a spiritual nature and of the obligations of Christian inspiration and friendship.

AREA ORGANIZATION

RESIDENT BISHOP—Frederick D. Leete
Secretary at the Office, Miss Hazel Funk

DISTRICT SUPERINTENDENTS

W. T. Arnold	O. W. Fifer	F. F. Thornburg
B. D. Beck	L. C. Jeffrey	R. H. Toole
L. C. Bentley	O. T. Martin	C. B. Whiteside
E. H. Boldrey	George H. Murphy	W. H. Whitlock
U. S. A. Bridge	J. E. Murr	W. W. Wiant
A. T. Briggs	C. L. Peterson	F. O. Wilson
W. M. Brown	J. T. Scull	J. J. Wilson
	Charles H. Smith	

OFFICIALS OF THE CONFERENCES

Indiana Conference

H. W. Baldridge..................Secretary C. M. Kroft..........................Treasurer
C. P. McKinney.................Statistician C. S. Black...........................Registrar

North Indiana Conference

Dorie V. Williams.................Secretary A. C. Wischmeier.................Treasurer
Arthur J. Armstrong.........Statistician M. O. Lester......................Registrar

Northwest Indiana Conference

F. O. Fraley.........................Secretary J. E. McCloud.....................Treasurer
H. M. Braun.....................Statistician Claude Young.....................Registrar

Southern Illinois Conference

W. H. Whitlock..................Secretary N. C. Henderson.................Treasurer
B. H. Batson....................Statistician W. E. Bennett......................Registrar

The Conferences

••••••••••••

THE INDIANA CONFERENCE
By H. C. Clippinger, D.D.

WHAT is now the Indiana Conference of the Methodist Episcopal Church, prior to 1832, was included in the Illinois Conference, and the territory covered by that conference included all of Indiana, a small part of Michigan, and a portion of Ohio. In 1832 the Indiana Conference was organized, and held its first session in New Albany, October 17, 1832, with a lay membership of 17,000 and sixty-five traveling preachers.

Methodism grew quite rapidly in those early days, and in 1844 the National Road was made a dividing line between two conferences, the North Indiana Conference and the Indiana Conference. Before this division there were 216 traveling preachers and 67,219 members. After the formation of the North Conference there remained to the Indiana Conference 110 traveling preachers, 285 local preachers and 35,686 members. In 1852 continued growth brought the number of traveling preachers to 159, the local preachers to 302, and the members to 39,271. Again the mother conference was divided and the Southeast Indiana Conference was formed, holding its first session in Rushville, October 6, 1852. Bishop Baker presiding, F. C. Holliday serving as secretary. It had a lay membership of 16,868. In 1876 the General Conference gave the Indiana and Southeast Indiana Conferences the authority to unite if they so desired. Such action was not taken, however, until 1895, when it was perfected at a session presided over by Bishop Mallalieu, at Central Avenue Church in Indianapolis. The lay membership was then reported in the conference minutes as 87,461 and R. A. Kemp was made secretary of the united body. He had served the Indiana Conference as secretary since 1881 and continued under the new plan until 1909, when he was succeeded by H. W. Baldridge, who still serves. The growth of the conference is indicated by the last statistical report in the minutes of 1927, which shows 295 preachers and probationers, with a lay membership of 116,882.

The Ninety-sixth annual session of the Indiana Conference was held in the new Irvington Church in Indianapolis, September 1927, Bishop Theodore S. Henderson of the Cincinnati Area presiding. J. B. Lathrop, 102 years old, is the senior member of the conference and resides in his retired relationship at Greensburg, where he has been engaged in business for many years. There is only one other conference in Methodism that has this distinction of having a member who has passed the century mark as to age.

By a change in boundary lines, DePauw University, formerly Indiana Asbury University, at Greencastle, has passed from the territory of the Indiana Conference to that of the Northwest Indiana Conference. This conference has always been a strong, loyal patron of the institution, which was established some ninety years ago, by the devoted pioneers of early Indiana Methodism.

The conference has made several contributions of men to the Episcopacy—notably, Bishop Ames, Bishop Simpson, first president of Asbury, Bishop Bowman, a later president, Bishop Hughes, and Bishop McConnell, recent Presidents of DePauw. The Indiana Conference has also furnished considerable editorial ability for our church publications. Bishop Matthew Simpson served a period of editorship of the Western Christian Advocate. B. F. Rawlins, J. J. Hight and E. Robb Zaring, were assistant editors of the Western Christian Advocate, the latter serving twelve years as editor of the Northwestern Christian Advocate. Wilbur F. Sheridan made a notable record as general secretary of the Epworth League, and has left a most lasting impression for good upon the young life of the church. "Win my chum" services were a part of his evangelistic program for the Epworth League to observe.

President Lemuel H. Murlin started on his career as a college president from the pastorate of the First Church, Vincennes, and his record of thirty-three years, as President of Baker University, Boston University, and DePauw University is unique.

Judge Asa Iglehart, a distinguished jurist of Evansville, was elected an alternate lay delegate to the General Conference of 1872 and 1884, meeting in Brooklyn and Philadelphia, respectively. The Iglehart descendants are loyal and generous supporters of Methodism, associated with Trinity Church, Evansville, maintaining the splendid record of the father and grandfather of the early history of the church. A contribution of $100,000 by the Igleharts in their home city has given this church a beautiful up-to-date stone building and organ chimes, making it one of the great modern church buildings of the middle west. F. C. Iglehart, a son of the judge, served the church a term as pastor and went east to serve successively several strong churches in New York. J. L. Pitner, once pastor of this church, left our conference for Hennepin Avenue, Minneapolis, and then to California, where he died.

J. E. Brant, a former secretary of our body, and Presiding Elder of the Evansville District, went from us to Kansas, where he became a prominent leader. His daughter, Mrs. Anna B. Adams, of Bloomington, served as conference treasurer for the Women's Foreign Missionary Society for thirty-three years.

I. N. Thompson, Hayden Hays, H. J. Talbott, T. H. Willis, M. S. Heavenridge, James Hill, J. H. Noble, Aaron Turner, are names that deserve honorable mention for leadership in the making of the record of this Conference. Space forbids a special tribute for these and others like them.

W. R. Halstead has had fifty-four years of effective service in the church, the most of these years given to service of marked leadership, in this conference as a district leader and representative of the hospital, pastor in leading churches and as a writer and author of books. He took a supernumerary relation at our last conference session.

John A. Ward has recently published a life story of his forty years of service in our conference. He retired in 1906. John A. Ward led our General Conference delegation to the Omaha session in 1892. W. R. Halstead, J. H. Ketcham were the delegates and W. H. Grim and John Poucher, alternates. All have died but the first two, Ward and Halstead. Halstead led the delegation to the Cleveland General Conference in 1896, and was a member of the delegation to the Los Angeles General Conference in 1904, and the New York General Conference in 1888.

The life of John Kiger by T. D. Welker is a very interesting volume concerning a strong leader of Indiana Methodism. He served as a presiding elder for thirty years, three terms on the New Albany District. He was a member of three General Conferences, and gave fifty years of service to our ministry.

John M. Walker has published a significant book on church

music, heralding a new epoch in the important place music holds in the regular worship services of the church.

John Poucher was a frequent contributor of special articles to the church press, and has left a notable record as a leader in the administrative and educational work of our conference. He was a member of the delegation representing our conference in the General Conference of 1884 at Philadelphia, with Alexander Martin and B. F. Rawlins. W. H. Grim and Aaron Turner were alternates. Alexander Martin, H. J. Talbott and W. R. Halstead were our delegates in 1888 to New York, John H. Ketcham and W. McK. Hester, alternates.

Charles E. Asbury in 1912 published a helpful book on "The Development of Christian Character" which is a valuable contribution for class study, as well as for individual study of the Bible on this theme. His wife is a leader in the Woman's Foreign Missionary Work of the church, and is favorably known throughout our conference. She led the lay delegation to our General Conference at Springfield in 1924, and is a member of the lay delegation to Kansas City in 1928.

Rev. J. L. Stout as superintendent of the Children's Home, and Rev. George M. Smith as superintendent of our Methodist Hospital work, deserve honorable mention in this article. Their leadership in these features of Indiana Methodism are closely associated with the development of the Indiana Conference.

The list of members of the Southeast Conference before the union with the Indiana Conference calls to mind a notable number of distinguished leaders, W. R. Lathrop, F. C. Holliday, Sampson Tincher, J. W. Millender, J. Tincher, J. W. Turner, M. B. Hyde, C. C. Edwards, J. H. Doddridge, T. G. Beharell, J. B. Lathrop, E. G. Wood, J. A. Sargent, J. S. Tevis, J. H. Bayliss, Editor Western Christian Advocate; G. L. Curtis, nineteen years secretary of the conference; E. L. Dolph, seven years secretary; L. D. Moore, three years secretary; J.P.D. John, President of DePauw University; J. W. Duncan, secretary for the Preachers' Aid Society, member of the Baltimore General Conference. M. B. Hyde, E. H. Wood, J. H. Doddridge and L. D. Moore are still living and are on the roll of retired preachers. Nearly every one of the list has served the church as presiding elder or district superintendent, and has had the honor of being a delegate to the General Conference in his day of service.

W. B. Collins was one of the youngest men ever made a presiding elder when assigned to the Vincennes District, following B. F. Rawlins. He made a notable record during his term, and the district advanced greatly under his leadership. After a transfer to the Kentucky Conference, where he built Trinity Church, Louisville, and another transfer to Detroit Conference, where he was made a district superintendent, and at the close of twenty-one years absence, he returned to the Indiana Conference in 1917, serving two years at Mt. Vernon and two years at Spencer. He retired in 1921, and now resides in California.

C. E. Bacon came to us from the North Indiana Conference in 1891 and was appointed to Trinity Church, Evansville. He has served Evansville, Connersville and Indianapolis, as superintendent, and has been secretary to the Federal Council of Churches. He has been a delegate to five General Conferences, has been a trustee of DePauw University for many years, served as a member of our Book Committee, and was in the hospital work as a trustee from its beginning. He closed his effective relationship in 1925, and with his wife resides in California.

W. McK. Hester, and T. G. Beharrell resided in New Albany after they superannuated. When J. E. Steele died, while in charge of the New Albany District, Wm. McK. Hester was put on the district to fill out the year. They have many relatives still living in New Albany, loyal supporters of Methodism in the city where the first conference session was held in 1832.

This notable Methodist center has entertained the conference more than any other city of the conference. It was the home of DePauw College for young women for many years, the property having been secured through the generosity of Washington C. DePauw, a great friend of education and a most loyal supporter of the general work of the church. His gift to Asbury, now DePauw University, made when its situation was very serious and critical, started that institution on its upward career. He served as a class leader, steward, and trustee, and was a leader of special meetings in the interest of holiness. He was a trustee and director in twenty-two colleges, universities, banks and corporations, and was a lay delegate to the General Conference of 1872 and 1876. He was born in 1822. For more than twenty-five years he refused to be a candidate for any public office. He refused the nomination for the governorship in 1872. He was very successful in business, and accumulated a large fortune for his day, using it wisely in the Lord's work, assisting churches and helping young men prepare for the ministry. The largest Sunday school in Southern Indiana was directed and supported by him for many years, in a large building in New Albany. Two sons, W. T. and Charles were associated with him in business in New Albany, and a daughter, Mrs. A. J. McIntosh and her family, resided in Salem, Indiana, for many years, finally removing to Indianapolis. Mr. and Mrs. A. J. McIntosh died a few years ago. The son, Newland T. led the lay delegation to the General Conference at Omaha in 1892. He was an alternate in 1888. Both sons, W. T. and Charles were graduates of Asbury. W.T. was a trustee of Trinity Church, New Albany, at the time of his death. A daughter, Mrs. E. V. Knight, is still a member of the church. Her husband, Col. Knight, succeeding Mr. DePauw as a trustee of DePauw University, still occupies that position. The charge built a $15,000 parsonage during the pastorate of Albert Hurlstone. Mr. De-Pauw and Hon. Alexander Dowling were trustees who gave generous support of time and money to this commendable enterprise. Mr. Dowling was a son-in-law of John Kiger and attorney for W. C. DePauw.

Judge Dowling was elected a member of the Supreme Court of Indiana and was one of the most talented judges who ever enjoyed that distinction. A fine, legal mind, a courteous Christian gentleman, a great friend to the ministry of his church, his record is a commendable one for laymen to emulate.

The conference session held at Jeffersonville in September, 1925, as noted elsewhere in this book, had a feature of great historical interest in a visit to Charlestown. It was in commemoration of the reconstruction and rededication of the "First Methodist Episcopal Log Church" built in Indiana. It was also the one hundredth anniversary of the session of the Illinois Conference held at Charlestown in 1825.

Meridian Street Church is the mother church of Methodism for Indianapolis and had a strong list of pastors in its eventful history. Bishop W. A. Quayle was one greatly beloved, Joshua Stansfield has a record of fifteen years' service in this pulpit. The present pastor, Virgil E. Rorer, has entered on his ninth year with this historic church.

THE NORTH INDIANA CONFERENCE

By Frank G. Browne, D.D.

Methodism set foot on Indiana soil as early as 1801 and came to stay. It is the purpose of this sketch to show how adventurously Methodism has "carried on" in that section of our commonwealth embraced within the limits of the North Indiana Conference since her territorial detachment from the Indiana Conference in 1844, and particularly since the creation of her blithe and comely neighbor, the Northwest Indiana Conference, in 1852.

Our conference held its first session in Berry Street Church, Fort Wayne, in September, 1844, Bishop Waugh presiding. It consisted of 105 preachers. Its six districts contained an aggregate membership, including probationers, of 27,563. Twelve men were admitted on trial, an encouraging augury of the unfailing supply of recruits that from year to year were to replenish and reinforce its ranks. Bishop and Mrs. Hamline were guests of the conference, as was also the Rev. Allen Wiley of the Indiana Conference. He was acquainted with the men and the field, for as presiding elder he had traveled the Madison District when it extended to the Wabash river and included the city of Fort Wayne. Bishop Waugh invited him into the meetings of the cabinet, and availed himself of Wiley's intimate knowledge of the men and the theater of their activities in making the appointments. Bishop Waugh wept with the preachers at the recital of their sorrows and hardships and rejoiced with them in their victories. His wise counsels, unaffected sympathy and impartiality in making their appointments inspired in them a splendid morale as they went forth to build their lives into the growing structure of the new conference.

The roads in the fall of the year were almost impassable, and preachers who lived at considerable distance from the seat of the conference started thither several days in advance of the date of the session. Many of them on horseback met at appointed centers and traveled together in companies like the ancient Jews on their annual pilgrimages to their great festivals at Jerusalem. The jokes and stories the preachers exchanged, the hymns they sang, the devotions they held in the homes of the people who kept them over night, the services they conducted and the sermons they preached in the churches on their way where in some instances a "two days meeting" had been arranged for in anticipation of their coming—all this in good fellowship and joyousness rivalled the "songs of degrees" with which the Jewish pilgrims beguiled the weariness and monotony of their journey to the city and house of the Lord.

The winter and spring of 1847-48 witnessed gracious and sweeping revivals. A meeting on the Peru circuit was reported to the Western Christian Advocate as "A powerful, high-rising, wide-spreading, onward-rolling, soul-saving, and God-fearing revival." The preacher in charge of Wabash mission which consisted of seventeen appointments, organized ten Sunday schools, and joyfully reported: "We have commenced to build meeting-houses." On completion of a new church at Romney the statement was issued: "The seats are free; the organ is of God's own making—the voices of the worshipping assembly." Rented pews and instrumental music in Indiana Methodism those days were taboo. A splendid new church at Valparaiso was described as "a snow white edifice." New churches were built at important points in the Kokomo mission, and at Anderson, Bristol, South Bend, Peru and Richmond. "Two days meetings" were often held and were seasons of refreshing. Quarterly meeting occasions were occasions indeed, beginning Friday night, continuing Saturday and Sunday, and closing Monday morning. People from all points on the charge attended. In love-feast they bore unfaltering testimony to their "comfortable assurance" of acceptance with the Lord and the reality of "that religion that happifies the soul." "The Elder" preached gloriously. When the invitation was given few stayed away from the table of the Lord. And from the "Quarterly" the people dispersed to their homes realizing that "it was good to be there." The camp-meeting was the most notable feature of the year. Practically it was an unsurpassed school of methods for young preachers, class-leaders, and exhorters, affording them frequent opportunities for the exercise of their gifts, and contact with the great preachers of the church. People in multitudes flocked to these centers of spiritual power. Those who came to scoff remained to pray. The saints of the Lord were strengthened with might by His Spirit in the inner man. The newly converted were confirmed in the faith. There were shouts

General *and* Institutional Officials

Charles C. Hall, Superintendent Southern Illinois Orphanage; Earl E. Harper, president Evansville College; John Paul, president Taylor University; C. Howard Taylor, secretary State and Area Councils: Raymond J. Wade, executive secretary World Service Commission; George M. Smith, superintendent Methodist Hospitals of Indiana; Cameron Harmon, president McKendree College; M. C. Hunt, director Wesley Foundation, Purdue; Blaine E. Kirkpatrick, secretary Epworth League; Clarence E. Flynn, director Wesley Foundation, Indiana University; Lemuel H. Murlin, president DePauw University: B. S. Hollopeter, secretary Methodist Memorial Home; William S. Bovard, secretary Board of Education; Ernest C. Wareing, editor Western Christian Advocate; Joseph L. Stout, superintendent Methodist Children's Home of Indiana.

of joy and victory in the camp at every gathering. Each annual assembly in the tented grove was eagerly looked forward to as a season of glorious fellowship and great refreshing from the presence of the Lord.

At the end of the second quadrennium after its organization, the conference had grown to such proportions that the brethren were cordially unanimous in the opinion that there should be another division of territory and another conference created to take care of the growing interests of Methodism in the northwestern part of the state. The General Conference of 1852 authorized the desired division, and accordingly the newly created Northwest Indiana Conference, under auspicious conditions, set up housekeeping for itself.

The first session of the new North Indiana Conference was held in Berry Street Church, Fort Wayne, in September, 1852, with Bishop Baker in the chair. It included six districts and had a total lay membership of 17,490 of which 2,697 were probationers. With abounding energy and hopefulness it entered upon the new era. Young men predominated in its ranks, and brought to the growing demands and responsibilities of the work in the charges and on the districts the vigor and buoyancy of youth. Its neighbors called it the "young men's conference," and jocosely remarked that "North Indiana takes boys and makes presiding elders of them." The "boys" gave themselves with unstinted devotion to the needs and claims that challenged their fidelity, and the field responded plenteously to their toil.

The intensity of feeling against "the unholy traffic in intoxicating liquors" was voiced in the temperance resolutions of the conference in 1853. The annual Indiana State Temperance Convention was held in Indianapolis in 1854. Twelve hundred delegates were there from all over the state. The leadership of Methodism in temperance reform was recognized by the election of Bishop Ames as president of the convention. Intemperance was not the only stalking evil that the conference at this period definitely and uncompromisingly assailed. It wielded a heavy cudgel against the iniquity of human slavery. A visitor to our conference at this time said: "The preachers are about as spirited and fearless as any body of men that can be found. They are young, hearty, warm-hearted and bold. They had a committee on slav-

ery, which very cooly brought in a report that in other places
would have produced spasms in the body ecclesiastic. It did not
excite the preachers. They did not talk much, but voted unanimously."

Members of the conference promptly responded to President
Lincoln's repeated calls for volunteer troops. Enlistments were
encouraged. The preachers were prominent in the "war meetings" where volunteers were called for, and their patriotic fervor
and eloquent appeals caused hundreds of men to rally to the defense of the flag. A number of the preachers who enlisted became company officers, and fifteen or more rendered invaluable
service as chaplains in camp, field and hospital. The preachers at
home loyally supported the war. What they did to inspire and
sustain the morale of loyal people it would take a chapter to relate.

Notwithstanding the absorbing war interest and constant work
at home for the relief and comfort of the soldiers through the
Sanitary and Christian Commissions, the church grew and pros-
pered. The dreadful ordeal through which the nation passed
deepened and intensified the spiritual life of the churches. As a
consequence there were gracious revivals all over the conference.
The conference missionary collections of 1865 were more than
three times what they were in 1861.

The conference benefited greatly by the observance of the one
hundredth anniversary of American Methodism in 1866. The
Methodist churches and conferences of the country united in the
centennial celebration. Appropriate services were held everywhere, at which thank-offerings were taken. It was a time for
contributions to all the manifold claims and interests of the Kingdom. Church debts were paid. Missions, church extension, work
among the destitute whites and freedmen in the South, increased
ministerial support, general and clerical education were vastly
promoted by the grateful gifts of our people, all of which evinced
one hundred per cent appreciation of the importance of the
meaningful anniversary.

The score of years extended from 1870 to 1890 is marked by
the progress of the conference, in almost all respects commensurate with the growth and prosperity of the country. The reactions from the Civil War stimulated business enterprise. The
population of the state greatly increased. New roads were opened, old ones repaired, bridges were built, money became plentiful,

the living conditions of the people were greatly improved, and the church in all her "temporalities" profited by the prosperity that prevailed. Numerous churches and parsonages of modern type were erected, old ones were made more commodious and inviting, circuits were reduced in size and a number of additional stations created, the preachers' salaries were very appreciably increased as were also contributions for the support of the superannuates. Women's work in the church, then and continuously since, has been magnificently carried on by the Women's Foreign and Home Missionary Societies. The Epworth League came into being and gathered strength during the last years of this period, destined as it was to be a mighty adjunct in making "our church a power in the world" and in helping it to love and cooperate with "every other church that exalts our Christ."

The conference sessions became highly notable occasions. Churches vied with each other in the offer of invitations to the conference to fix upon their city or town as the seat of its next session. The conference program, reports, and daily proceedings crowded the columns of and were eagerly featured by the local papers. The annual visits to the conference assembled of the representative men of the church, the general secretaries, editors, missionaries, and sometimes of a bishop in addition to the one presiding; the thrilling anniversaries of the great societies when Durbin, Reid and Eddy with tongue of flame pressed home the needs and claims of our growing missions abroad, when the soldierly Hartzell graphically described the destitution of the South which the Freedmen's Aid Society was valiantly endeavoring to mitigate, and the inimitable McCabe, champion of church extension, sang and shouted his way into the hearts and purses of preachers and people—all these were mountain-peak experiences to be cherished and talked about for years to come.

The period of the natural gas boom was fraught with tremendous material advantage to the North Indiana Conference, and yet it was not an unmixed blessing. The reactions that the churches in many places experienced with the subsidence of that economic movement were afflictive, if not disastrous. On the whole the churches that belonged to the "gas belt" and were dependent on it, pulled up to advanced lines which with exceptions here and there they have since maintained and carried forward. Churches outside that flamboyant region, little affected by the fluctuations that seized it, held steadily on their way, registering each year the results of continuous and vigorous growth.

In its support of those claims that relate to the kingdom of God, during the first quarter of the twentieth century the conference has made a highly creditable and in some items a very remarkable record. It is to be noted that commendable interest has been manifest in our local history. Churches have collected and put in condition for preservation authentic data for adequate sketches of our societies, ministers and leading laymen. As a part of this movement the graves of our deceased ministers have been located and suitably marked. Our Epworth League chapters have led in this labor of love. This too has been a period of vast advancement in strictly conference enterprises, as the records of the Preachers' Aid Society attest, as does also the existence of Epworth Forest Institute, the Fort Wayne Methodist Hospital and the Methodist Memorial Home for the Aged at Warren. To these splendid institutions will soon be added the Bashor orphanage which is in process of financing. In "World Service" North Indiana has maintained forefront alignment with the great conferences of Methodism.

Carlyle said, "History is the essence of innumerable biographies." The history of the North Indiana Conference from the beginning is embodied in the lives and achievements of its outstanding men. We can advert to only a few of them: Augustus Eddy and William H. Goode, bishops in everything except the name; Milton Mahin, poised and resourceful, valiant for the truth, who put to flight the armies of the aliens in his numerous and memorable debates with immersionists and Universalists; R. D. Robinson, a big man, with girth of brain and heart as great as that of his body, college president, typical old-time presiding elder, at his best in a great sermon Sunday morning of quarterly meeting in a crowded country church, or on the conference floor in an impassioned plea for a young preacher up for admission on trial who had failed to make passing grades in some of his studies, "Give me my boy!" shouted in sonorous tones and with melting emotion, touched the preachers' hearts and elicited thunderous applause; S. C. Cooper, Samuel Brenton, W. S. Birch, M. H. Mendenhall, F. T. Simpson, T. Stables, H. N. Herrick, leaders for years, honored and beloved by their brethren for their statesmanlike wisdom and sagacity; C. G. Hudson, accomplished scholar, conference secretary for sixteen years; W. D. Parr, variously and brilliantly gifted, champion of church extension; L. J. Naftzger, pastor-evangelist, conference secretary for ten years; Madison Swadener, prohibition-advocate whose labors and influence were nation-wide. To these must be added a few of our many noble laymen who contributed in innumerable ways to the success of our ministers: George Milburn, A. C. Swayzee, J. H. Baker, C. C. Binkley, D. G. Linville, W. C. Chafee, G. W. H. Kemper, Thomas Redding, Hugh Dougherty.

> "As a bird each fond endearment tries,
> To tempt its new-fledged offspring to the skies,
> They tried each art, reproved each dull delay,
> Allured to brighter worlds and led the way."

Until kerosene lamps came into general use, evening services were announced for "early candle-lighting." While the preacher droned, as sometimes he did, and the people dozed, a meek brother quietly made the rounds and snuffed the wicks that flared and fell in the "dim religious light."

The general rules were punctually read once a quarter. The cotillion was the popular dance in social circles, and preachers were wont to rebuke giggling young folks in stern and stereotyped phrase for "whirling in the giddy mazes of the cotillion."

Instrumental music in the church for many years was a sensitive question. In some localities it caused dissension, the violence of which is suggested in the phrase by which it was described— the "organ war."

Inveterate prejudice against preaching with manuscript was voiced by a venerable steward who was wont to say "a writ sermon is no sermon for me." Methodists wanted preaching "hot off the griddle."

Conference examinations were oral, and far from as elaborate and exacting as they are today when all tests are written, and the work of the student is subjected to kindly but critical inspection.

Methodist history, local or ecumenical, would be incomplete without adequate record and reference to conference boundaries. Said a witty bishop: "Methodist preachers never quarrel among themselves except concerning conference boundaries and sanctification." The equanimity of our conference was violently disturbed when by action of the General Conference of 1868 our section of Marion County was made a part of the Southeast Indiana Conference. Far be it from this historian to allege that studied adroitness in the General Conference delegates of the Southeast Indiana Conference enabled them to perpetrate this bit of spoliation. The hurt has long since healed. And now the North Indiana Conference may be pardoned if she feels that the Indianapolis Churches of which she was bereft would not be so great and flourishing in the waxing splendor of the twentieth century had they not been fostered by her maternal care during their infantile and adolescent years.

"The old order changeth, yielding place to new,
And God fulfills Himself in many ways."

The North Indiana Conference faces the future with the light of the morning on her brow and the strength and passion of unfaltering faith in her soul. She has "good news to tell," a glad and affirmative message, and in the spirit of the evangelical commission and Frances Havergal's noble hymn, she can be depended on, joyously and convincingly to "tell it out."

THE NORTHWEST INDIANA CONFERENCE

By William Howard Hickman, D.D., fifty-five years in the conference.

The Northwest Indiana Conference was organized in Terre Haute, September 8, 1852. It covers less than one-fourth of the state and is divided into three parts, fertile prairie, timber lands, and water waste. The early citizens came from the East and North, with a liberal number from the southern states.

At the first session vision and leadership were displayed. The members came from the North Indiana Conference, and had training in conference affairs. The conference was well organized. It entered nearly all the fields of church work.

Cousin says in his philosophy that "The great men of a nation sit on the front seats" so a few men of the Northwest Indiana Conference sit on the front seats of the conference and are in world-wide Methodism. Within this territory three men lived and wrought, who are known around the world: Lew Wallace, John Clark Ridpath, and Clem Studebaker, Methodist laymen. Lew Wallace was a personal friend whom I knew for thirty years; John Clark Ridpath was my teacher in college; Clem Studebaker was my counsel and support in the darkest days DePauw University ever passed.

Three of the men who were present in the first roll call of '52 have been present themselves or had descendents present in every conference since. The Wood family, the Hargraves, and the Greens are examples. Tom Wood, the son of Aaron, was a missionary and diplomat in South Africa for more than forty years. The son of Moses Wood, after serving as pastor and presiding elder, is now chaplain of the Northern penitentiary. The Hargraves have been present at every conference and are present now. A brother to Nelson Green, James, served in this conference many years with marked success. A son of Nelson Green is now pastor in a sister conference.

At this conference session steps were taken to support Indiana Asbury University. The roll was called and ministers responded in personal gifts. The first subscription I ever made was to Asbury University when a student. It took me years to pay it off, as it drew 10% interest. At this conference a man was put in the field to solicit for the building of a high school in Terre Haute. A man was put in the field for a male and female college at La-Porte. A proposition was submitted to build a special school for the training of ministers' children. At this first session three men offered themselves for the mission field.

The greater number in the conference, however, were like the greater number in our conference now—men who went to their work with a conviction and sacrifice, "Diligent in business, fervent in spirit, serving the Lord." The ambition of every man was to have a great revival, build a church and take in territory.

Those were the days of great camp meetings. The people would come for many miles in wagons and on horseback, camping for days. The old time camp meeting orator would lead in evangelism. The people sang with fervor, conversions by scores were had, and shouts of triumph were heard.

One of the chief things in the reports on the conference floor was the number of conversions and members added to the church. The pastor was measured more by that report than the amount of money raised.

There were few newspapers, few railroads, little communication beyond the neighborhood, few people living in more than humble homes, few schools, few churches, and nothing to interest the people in national affairs except politics.

One-fourth of the city of Indianapolis had fallen within the bounds of this conference, and it was called a "mission field." Steps were taken to erect a church, Roberts Chapel; a pastor was appointed; and $1,000 was promised toward the building.

The order in conference sessions has changed but little in these fifty years, but the business method and the things stressed have changed much. Sixty years ago it was expected that subjects of wide interest would be debated on the conference floor. I was a member of a general conference when the conference debated for two weeks the question of admitting women. At the conclusion of those debates one of the most distinguished men of this nation, himself a great statesman and debater said, "I know the House of Representatives, I know the Senate, I have heard debates in both, but I have never heard as skillful handling and clean cut arguments—ready answers on constitutional questions as these Methodist preachers displayed in the debates I heard."

The annual conferences in those days furnished the matter and the platform for training debaters. We have lost much by not having some such debates in these days. I learned much from these debates. The debaters, sometimes in the heat of feeling stand out in my memory so clearly I cannot be mistaken when I call them great. We have lost something—as well as gained something—by the orderly and painfully dignified brief and crowded conference session. It must be said, however, that there are more men taking part, and the spirit of democracy is more apparent in the conference session today than fifty years ago.

Conference Door Protected.

The protection against men ill-fitted to enter the conference is better now than it was fifty years ago. To be admitted now a man has to be almost as perfect as the Jew for membership in the Sanhedrin. Family background, age, education, religious fitness, family ties, personal habits, doctrinal belief, all these and more are put into various questions and the candidates catechized, graded, and reported on the conference floor. Then in the candidate's absence, questions are asked before the final vote is taken. Seventy years ago a few things were stressed more than now, such as, a definite Christian experience and a call to the ministry. One could get by with little education, but he could not get by without answering certain very definite questions about his experience, belief, and purpose as to obedience and consecration to his work. Then he could use tobacco, now he can not. Then he could have age on his head, now he cannot. Then it was in his favor not to have a wife, now it is against him. Then it was a bit discreditable not to have a revival and ingathering. He would not generally bring up his apportionments in full and this was not a surprise. Now he may go through the year without a revival, without gathering in a soul, provided he makes a creditable showing in his reports, which are often running over, and has acquitted himself like a Christian gentleman, and stands well with his young people and the community generally.

The Methodist preacher then was known as the foe of liquor traffic, but not any more so than he is now. When the conference was organized the slavery question was at the center of a great approaching storm, but was avoided in open debate, especially by men who were candidates for favors. The Methodist preacher was opposed to slavery. But the methods of doing away with slavery were debatable. So in these latter years the method of destroying the liquor traffic was debatable, but a few of us began forty years ago to make it our business to bring this question to the front, in season and out, till prohibition of the liquor traffic went into the Constitution. Then we were divided. Now we are one for the law and the Gospel.

Aaron Wood

Aaron Wood was a man of medium size, smooth face except a little side beard, a square chin, big mouth, long stiff upper lip, deep set eyes, high forehead, prominent nose—a Gladstone face. A voice not heavy, but strong and penetrating. He had an air of independence and courage, was a wide reader, had a tenacious memory, was an original thinker, and was gifted with that surprise power that challenges attention and commands in leadership. He was not especially fond of the fine arts, but was a natural philosopher, a kind of Ben Franklin. What he lacked in magnetism he made up in clearness and unique statements. He had a remarkable faculty for dates and names. He was very frank in his opinions. On the conference floor a young man was up for admission. Dr. Wood said, "I knew this man's father and mother. His mother was a sensible woman, his father had little sense. This man takes after his father. I don't think he is fit for our ministry." The young man was not admitted.

At a camp meeting he was on the pulpit committee. He came to me and said, "Hickman, I want you to preach at 2:00." I said, "I can't do it, I am not prepared." He replied, "A Methodist preacher ought to be ready to die or preach, and so far as I am concerned I don't care which you do." I preached that afternoon. He was a pastor at eighty-three in my district when we put him away, crowned with age and honor.

Richard Hargrave

Richard Hargrave was the opposite of Dr. Aaron Wood in everything except as a camp meeting orator. His mind was deep and narrow, his body large and commanding. He had a heavy voice with the sweep of an army trumpet. He was not broad in his reading, except in the field of theology. He did not have many themes upon which to preach but in those he did present, especially in the field of holiness, he was the strong preacher of his day. Silent, serious and solemn, he was a great camp meeting orator. He would reach heights of oratory and emotion moving the multitude like wind bending wheat. He possessed a dignity that kept him in a class to himself and approachable and loveable, yet never trifling or foolish. He was leaving my home on a winter day when he stood silent in the door, with his long gray locks, full white beard, cane in hand. Looking up into the skies, he said, "Brother, row for the harbor." It was the last I saw of Richard Hargrave, prophet of the old school.

Samuel Godfrey

Samuel Godfrey was of French extraction, born in a cabin not chinked, the fire in the middle of the house. His early education was derived from nature in the forests. He was a probationer when the conference was organized, but would have been discontinued next year for going to a circus and playing marbles, but for the pleading of his presiding elder. In the heat of the debate next day the Godfrey case was overlooked. He took his family and went to Asbury University and graduated. He was of medium size and sallow complexion with black, stringy hair, black beard, high forehead, and a large yellow eye like a cat. He was a bit sloven in dress, with a soft swinging walk like an Indian. He was gifted in imagination. He could see the beauty in nature, the harmony and purpose in design. Like Wordsworth, he could put his visions and pictures into frames of speech. He could see the absurd and ridiculous, the sham and cunning, and could describe them like Byron. He had the logic of John Stewart Mill and the biting sarcasm of Dean Swift. His emotions were so controlled that no one could read his feelings. He had a memory that held everything with which he charged it. He had a command of the English tongue like Henry W. Grady, and could express the shades of meaning like Homer. He was a converted man, and saw God everywhere and communed with Him.

He did not have to learn to preach. He was licensed and told he had to preach that afternoon. He went to the deep woods and returned on time. Dr. John L. Smith told me he sat behind Godfrey and had to stuff his mouth with his handkerchief to keep silent when Godfrey went to the top. When he would reach his heights there was on his face a shy smile like a pale sunbeam on a snowbank. He hated hypocrisy and sham. He would handle both with ridicule. In his district was a church that believed in immersion as essential to salvation. Some of the Methodists were persuaded to go that way. At a quarterly meeting he held up in ridicule the idea of taking God's chickens and turning them into ducks. This created excitement. On his return the church and yard were filled. A man stood by the door as Dr. Godfrey entered, and handed him a paper which Dr. Godfrey read from the pulpit just as it was written. It was a challenge to debate baptism. With an expression of scorn he said, "I disdain to debate anything with any man who will spell God with a little 'g.'" He made his sermons with a fishing pole in his hand or sitting on a log, lost and motionless for hours.

John L. Smith

Large in body and mind, John L. Smith was a church statesman. In the field of politics he would have been a great diplomat and constitutional lawyer. He was converted and called to the ministry. The primeval forest, the unorganized settlements, and the human clay offered a field for a leader and builder, and John L. Smith was both. Limited in education, but with the will of a Caesar, he studied books, men, and the signs of the times. He knew men and made fast friends. He was an example of courage, industry, and sacrifice. He always had revivals and was a great church builder. In one town he gathered a small membership and built a church. But to do this he borrowed a horse and wagon, and hauled the lumber and brick himself. The hod carriers struck, and he carried the hod till the building was finished. He was a great advocate of higher education, and took a leading part in building Methodist schools. He was in the General Conference many times and was prominent among great men. He lived a long life which had a serene and cloudless ending.

John H. Hull

John H. Hull excelled all others in the spirit of evangelism. A man of splendid physique, tall and commanding presence, black eyes and hair like the raven, and a voice of remarkable sweep and power. He was a leader of men and a genius in constructive statesmanship. On into old age he kept the spirit of young manhood, and was always up to date in the affairs of church and state. He was in demand as a station preacher after his eyesight was gone. He was the ablest exhorter I ever knew. This talent to exhort is an important one. It is a wonderful power to enlist men for the Kingdom. It was cultivated by our fathers, but is little used by our younger ministers, and in this failure is a great loss. Of the 443 men on the conference roll, 181 have departed, answering the call to come up higher.

These five men were in the original organization and are given as specimens of an heroic age. Many of these men were great builders of the Kingdom. Bishop Joyce was born, bred, and came to distinction in this conference. Others I would mention but time and space prohibit me.

THE SOUTHERN ILLINOIS CONFERENCE

By W. C. Walton, Ph.D., Professor in McKendree College.

John Wesley declared, "The world is my parish". Today Methodism is literally world wide. But while it extends over much of the earth's surface it is not of equal intensity in every locality. The story of Methodism may be told as an international epic, covering the civilized nations and the mission fields, or the narrative may be confined to certain spots. In this account we shall tell of one of the important spots. Geographically the Southern Illinois Conference covers about one fourth the area of the Prairie State, including almost thirty-six counties and a total population of approximately 980,000 people. There is an actual membership of 60,000 Methodists in the conference, and if we allow for a Methodist constituency of twenty-five per cent additional, we see that almost one in ten of the people in this region has some relation to Methodism.

The story of this one conference cannot be told without telling much of others also, for as "No man liveth to himself" neither does any Methodist conference. The specific history of the Southern Illinois Conference does not reach back farther than 1852 when it was separated from the Illinois Conference and set up in business for itself in the field where this same Methodist church had already been doing business for more than half a century. First, let us trace the chain of title of the different conferences which have held this territory. When Methodism crossed the Allegheny Mountains it appeared for a time, only as the unorganized results of the spontaneous and unrestricted labors of the Methodist circuit riders; but in 1796 the General Conference gave the designation "Western Conference" to the whole Mississippi valley so far as there was any Methodism in it. It included Kentucky and Tennessee, and the Illinois Country, where the Roman Catholic missionaries had already been working for a century. Until 1812 Illinois was in the Western Conference. In that year the Tennessee Conference was organized. It included the territory of Illinois. In 1816 the Missouri Conference was organized at Shiloh, Illinois, with Bishop McKendree as presiding officer. It included the territory of Missouri, Illinois and the western half of Indiana. The first session of this great conference was held within the present territory of the Southern Illinois. In 1824 the Illinois Conference was organized at Union Grove near Summerfield, also in the present area of the Southern Illinois Conference. It included the entire states of Illinois and Indiana. In 1832 the state of Indiana was cut off and organized into the Indiana Conference. In 1840 the northern portion was separated and organized into the Rock River Conference. In 1852 the southern portion was separated and organized into the Southern Illinois Conference. Therefore the historic territory which this conference now occupies has belonged successively to the Western, the Tennessee, the Missouri, and the Illinois conferences. This region contains the sites of all the earliest settlements of the state which were the abode of white people, such as Cahokia, Kaskaskia, Fort Chartres, and others. It was through this territory that Colonel George Rogers Clark made his famous expedition during the Revolutionary War, in which he captured Kaskaskia and Vincennes, and wrested a vast area from the British and placed it in the possession of the Americans. In 1790 the first county in Illinois was organized and named for Governor St. Clair. About the same time Methodism began to find its way into Illinois, and, of course, it had its beginnings in St. Clair county, which at first occupied the whole southern end of the state. The first Methodist to live in Illinois of whom we find any record was Captain Joseph Ogle. He came from Virginia to Illinois in 1785 and lived first in the American Bottom and afterward a few miles north of Belleville. The first Methodist preacher to visit Illinois was Rev. Joseph Lillard, who was then a traveling preacher or missionary. During his temporary stay he gathered the few scattered Methodists into a class and appointed Captain Ogle as their leader. This class, formed in 1793, was the first Methodist class in the state, though it can hardly be called an organized church. The first Methodist preacher to live in Illinois was Rev. Hosea Rigg, a local preacher, who came from Pennsylvania in 1796 and settled in the American Bottom. Finding the class of which Captain Ogle had been appointed leader three years before in a disorganized condition, he gathered together as many Methodists as he could find and preached to them himself, and again placed them in Captain Ogle's charge. Among them we find the following names on record: Joseph Ogle and family, Peter Casterline and family, and William Murray, an Irishman. A few years later Mr. Rigg moved to the Turkey Hill settlement southeast of Belleville, and Captain Ogle to Ridge Prairie, west of O'Fallon. Here another class was formed with the Captain again as leader. It usually met in the Ogle home. Besides the Ogle family it included the family of William Scott of Turkey Hill and others, making a total of nineteen members. This class was afterward merged into the Shiloh church.

In 1803 Mr. Rigg went to the session of the Western Conference held at Mt. Gerizim, Kentucky, to ask for a preacher for the Illinois country. As a result of his petition the Illinois Mission was formed and Benjamin Young was appointed its first missionary. At the end of the year he reported to the conference a membership of sixty-seven. His mission embraced all the settlements from the mouth of the Kaskaskia to Wood River. One of his preaching places was the home of Squire Reynolds, the father of Governor John Reynolds, a short distance east of Kaskaskia. Another was New Design, just south of where Waterloo now stands. The Turkey Hill settlement, started by William Scott in 1787, contained a number of Methodists, and their preaching place was the home of Captain Ogle, in Ridge Prairie. Later it was Shiloh. Another preaching place was the Goshen settlement a few miles south of the present city of Edwardsville, founded by the Gillhams and the Whitesides in 1802. In 1804 the Western Conference met in the same place as the year previous, and was presided over by William McKendree, though he was not yet a bishop, since Bishop Asbury was kept away by illness. Rev. Joseph Oglesby was appointed to the Illinois Mission. Dr. Leaton says of him, "No history of Methodism in the Mississippi Valley can be complete which does not speak largely of the labors of Joseph Oglesby". At the close of the year he reported the membership in Illinois increased to one hundred twenty. In 1805 the Illinois Mission was called the Illinois Circuit. It was a part of the Cumberland District, of which William McKendree was Presiding Elder. Charles R. Matheny was appointed to the circuit that year, but we have no record of his work.

In the spring of 1806 Jesse Walker made a visit to the Illinois country with Presiding Elder McKendree, just to see what it was like. He was delighted with it and expressed the wish that he might work in that field. So in the fall of 1806 he was appointed

Superintendents *of* Indianapolis Area Districts

Northwest Indiana

JOHN J. WILSON   OTTO T. MARTIN   BERT D. BECK

ALBERTUS T. BRIGGS

Indiana Conference

LAWRENCE C. JEFFREY   ORIEN W. FIFER   GEORGE H. MURPHY

J. E. MURR   EDWIN H. BOLDREY   R. H. TOOLE   JOHN T. SCULL

to the Illinois Circuit. He returned to his home after conference, arriving at noon one day, and the next day at ten o'clock he had everything ready to start, with his wife and two daughters, for his new field of labor. It was a distance of nearly two hundred miles which they traveled on horseback. After a weary journey of several days they arrived at the Turkey Hill settlement near Belleville. His parsonage was an old log cabin belonging to Brother Scott. It had a plank floor and a stick chimney, with a hearth so low that the edge of the floor made seats for all the family as they sat around the fire. Leaving his family in this humble home he began to travel his state-wide circuit. On New Year's eve at the beginning of the year 1807 he held a "watch-night meeting", probably the first ever held in Illinois, and in connection with this meeting he held the first "Love-feast". In April 1807 he held the first camp meeting ever held in Illinois, in the Goshen settlement near Edwardsville. There were three preachers present, Jesse Walker, Charles R. Matheny, and Hosea Rigg. It was a time of power and there were a number of conversions. At times many of those present were affected with that strange phenomenon called "the jerks". In July of the same year another camp meeting was held at Three Springs, later known as Shiloh. This meeting is of peculiar historic interest because it resulted in the organization of the first permanent Methodist church in Illinois. When Shiloh Church celebrated its Centennial in 1907, much interesting history was brought to light. Some details which had been made a matter of record by Rev. James Lemen, a Baptist preacher of that community, were furnished by his son, Mr. James B. Lemen, and this made it possible to give a good account of these early events in the booklet which was published just after the celebration.

On June 10, 1807, the class convened at Captain Ogle's in a business session, and voted to hold a camp meeting and build a meeting house at Shiloh Grove, also known as Three Springs, because of the springs in the valley just below the camp ground. This was a central location for most of the class and they thought it would be the most suitable place for a permanent house of worship. Before the meeting began the members cut and hauled a part of the logs for the church and some of these were used temporarily for a platform and seats during the camp meeting.

On July 26, the Presiding Elder, William McKendree, arrived

and the meeting began. McKendree and Walker were the preachers. The meeting lasted eleven days and resulted in a great revival. On the last day, August 6, Captain Ogle's class, together with a number of the new converts, was organized into a church by Presiding Elder McKendree. There were forty-six members in the new church. Thus was Methodism permanently established in the state of Illinois. The church which was erected after the meeting closed was a log structure eighteen by twenty-two in size. This was replaced by a brick building in 1819, and this by a larger brick in 1875. The last mentioned was dedicated by Bishop Bowman and is still in use. The congregation is small, because the region has been largely taken over by a foreign population which Methodism has not been able successfully to absorb. It is a part of the O'Fallon charge, and hence the name Shiloh does not appear in the minutes, but nevertheless on this same spot has been maintained a house of worship with a regular pastor for a hundred and twenty years continuously. This can be said of no other place in Illinois Methodism. The Methodist preacher of the early days was not expected to revel in luxury, as evidenced by the minutes found in an old quarterly conference record book now in McKendree College library. The record shows that at a quarterly meeting held at Shiloh in 1833 the estimating committee brought in a report recommending the following allowance for the support of the pastor and his wife for the ensuing year:

Twenty pounds coffee	$ 4.00
Twenty pounds sugar at 10c	2.00
Four hundred lbs. beef and pork	10.00
Ten bushels cornmeal at 50c	5.00
Three hundred pounds flour	7.50
House rent, $1.50 per month	18.00
Corn to feed horse	7.50
Fodder, 200 bundles	2.00
Wood, six cords	6.00
Vegetables	3.00
Salt, pepper, and spice	1.00
Butter	2.50
Total	$68.50

This report was amended after discussion, and the corn and fodder were stricken out on the ground that they were not "table expenses". The allowance of sugar was raised from twenty to forty pounds, the flour to four hundred pounds, and the salt, pepper, and spice to two dollars. This raised the total of the year's allowance to $73.00. There is no record to show how the horse was fed that year, since that was left to the ingenuity of the circuit rider.

By 1811 the work had grown so much that there were two districts in the Illinois territory, the Illinois and the Wabash. In 1812 the Tennessee Conference was organized and these two districts became a part of it. Peter Cartwright was Presiding Elder of the Wabash District in 1812. In 1816 the first session of the Missouri Conference was held at Shiloh. Although it was in Illinois it was central to the territory included in the conference. Bishop McKendree came to hold the conference from Vincennes, where an armed and mounted guard of Methodist pioneers met him and escorted him over the St. Louis-Vincennes trail to Shiloh. This was probably his first visit to Shiloh since he had held the camp meeting and organized the church there nine years before. In 1824 the work had grown to such an extent that it was thought wise to divide the Missouri Conference into two and let the Mississippi river be a dividing line between them. This was provided for in the General Conference of 1824, and the first session of the Illinois Conference was held at Union Grove, near Summerfield, only about ten miles from Shiloh, and in the heart of the territory now occupied by the Southern Illinois Conference. The meeting was held at the home of William Padfield. The first session was held on Saturday, October 23, 1824, with only eleven members present, but by the following Monday there were thirty-three present. The journal was signed by Bishop Roberts, though both McKendree and Soule were there. Peter Cartwright intended to be there and was on his way with his family from Kentucky to Illinois, but in one of their camping places in the woods the camp fire at the foot of a tree burned it off at the base and it fell on one of the sleeping children and suddenly crushed the life out of the little girl. The delay caused by this accident made Cartwright too late for the conference, but he became a member of it and spent the remainder of his ministerial life in that conference. By this time the tide of immigration was beginning to surge in upon the broad prairies of Illinois, and Methodism was expanding beyond the bounds of the region that could be called

southern Illinois.   Cartwright made his home in Sangamon County, and his ministry ranged more or less over the whole state.
Jesse Walker carried Methodism into Chicago as early as 1830.
From the time of the organization of the Illinois Conference the
center of Illinois Methodism, as well as of the general populace,
moved gradually northward until in 1852 it was thought that the
cause would be best served by dividing this great conference into
two.   So the original field of Illinois Methodism was cut off and
organized into the Southern Illinois Conference.   Its heritage
was rich in receiving most of the historic spots which Methodism
now cherishes as treasured possessions, and most priceless of them
all is McKendree College at Lebanon.

The first session of the Southern Illinois Conference was held
at Belleville and opened on Wednesday, October 27, 1852. Bishop
Ames presided and Rev. James Leaton, then a member of the faculty at McKendree, was secretary. Edward R. Ames had been the
first Principal of Lebanon Seminary, which later became McKendree College, and at Lebanon he was licensed to preach and joined
the ranks of the circuit riders. It would seem appropriate for
him to visit the scene of his earlier labors, now only twelve miles
away; but we have no means of knowing whether he did or not.

There were in 1852 thirty-nine full members of the conference and sixteen probationers.   At that first session ten others
were received on trial.   That gave a conference roll of sixty-five.
There were five districts, forty-eight charges, one hundred and
seventeen churches, twenty-eight parsonages, one hundred and
eighty-four Sunday schools, and fourteen thousand nine hundred
and forty-eight members.   Statistics show that the population of
the conference area at that time was 137,563.   So there was one
Methodist for every ten people and a few extra for good measure.
Among the men on that original conference roll who afterward
occupied places of leadership in the church might be mentioned
Norman Allyn, James B. Corrington, Thomas A. Eaton, James
Leaton, James A. Robinson, Jotham A. Scarritt, and John Van
Cleve.

Southern Illinois is noted for the production of young preachers.   In the three-quarters of a century of its history the Southern Illinois Conference has received on trial seven hundred and
thirty-six young men.   Not all of these were received into full
membership, but many of them are accounted for by transfer.

This conference has never been distinguished for high salaries. When a man attains a position of leadership he is often influenced by offers of a much better living for his family and an equal opportunity to do good, to change to some field where there is greater wealth or where the church is more accessible than it is in Southern Illinois. Literally scores have transferred to the Illinois Conference which is still our neighbor on the north, and many to other conferences in all parts of the country. This conference prides itself on its leadership in various reforms, but especially on the fact that in 1868 it passed a rule requiring its new members to sign the tobacco pledge, several years before it was required by the General Conference.

In 1902 the conference celebrated its semi-centennial. There were at that time four of the charter members still living. Thomas A. Eaton, George W. Waggoner, Hiram Sears, and Jotham A. Scarritt. Of these only the last named was in a state of health which permitted him to be present, but Dr. Scarritt preached a most interesting Semi-Centennial sermon, recounting the victories and the progress of fifty years. He portrayed the conditions of the early times by recounting some of his own experiences, which we have not space to reproduce here except to say that from Alton he went to conference at Mt. Carmel, traveling twice across the state on horseback, and then moved to Walnut Hill, his new charge, more than half way across the state, in wagons furnished by Methodist farmers, who always donated such services to the preacher. The preachers' salaries of that day averaged less than $300 a year. Not until 1865 did any charge pay as much as $1,000. Cairo was the first charge to reach this figure. Now there are a score of $3,000 charges, while the maximum salary goes above $5,000.

From the beginning the conference was patriotic and hated slavery. At the opening of the civil war the members stood as one man for the national cause. Many of them left their charges for the time and joined the Union Army, some as chaplains, and others as officers or private soldiers. It has been estimated that nearly half the able bodied men in the conference were at some time during the war in some form of military service. During the World War, under the plan the Government followed, not many preachers were called into the army camps; but many preachers' sons were. Methodism was splendidly represented in

the war by the Southern Illinois boys. The Misses May Paul and
Mary Olive prepared a service flag for the conference in the summer of 1918. They sewed over 5,000 stars on a huge banner
which was raised in the church at Greenville where the conference met that year. It may now be seen at McKendree College.

Besides McKendree College, the history of which will be re-
counted separately, the conference has other institutions which it
has founded and fostered and of which it may justly be proud.
Among these are the Holden Hospital at Carbondale, where the
best of medical and surgical service may be obtained, and free service is furnished to Methodist preachers or members of their families.

Another is the Old Folks' Home at Lawrenceville, which has a
new $100,000 plant, where the evening of life is made comfort-
able for aged ones who are otherwise alone in the world. Another
is the orphanage at Mt. Vernon, where hundreds of unfortunate
children are given care and Christian training till they can be
placed in good private homes where they will grow into good
citizens and useful men and women.

In the last half century the conference has invested hundreds
of thousands of dollars in new churches. Now there is hardly a
town of any size, but has a substantial, and in many cases an ele-
gant Methodist church. According to the latest statistics the
conference has four hundred and sixty-four church buildings
valued at $4,418,000, and two hundred and seventeen parsonages
worth $634,850. The conference pays annually $423,330 for
ministerial support, and $181,212 for the various organized ben-
evolences of the church. Methodism is fairly well established in
Southern Illinois. It has accomplished much in its more than
a century of history in this region. But there is still much to do.
The more than two hundred members of the Southern Illinois
Conference are still fighting the forces of evil and diligently try-
ing to build up the Kingdom of God in this the southern portion
of our great state of Illinois.

The Districts

············

BLOOMINGTON DISTRICT, INDIANA CONFERENCE

By Edwin H. Boldrey, D.D., Superintendent.

ALMOST any building material the nation needs is produced in the Bloomington district, whether stone, brick, cement, or wood. Its mines and rivers provide light, heat and power. Annually many thousands find health and strength at its mineral springs. Its rugged hills and rolling prairies give inspiration to multitudes of lovers of "God's great out of doors." Matching all this is a wealth of humanity by whose magic skill hills of stone are transformed into cottages, sky-scrapers or temples; forests into furnishings; and veins of coal and rivers of water into comforts and luxuries. Much of this is wrought by people called Methodists. These, desiring to keep the spiritual above the material, have builded throughout the district a hundred houses for worship ranging from tiny churches in wildwoods to temples of stone enduring as the hills. It is impossible to indicate the spiritual gains resulting from this effort save as they have sought to consecrate the results of the labors of their hands to the support of the various phases of God's cause. Whatever their achievement for good, the glory is given to God. Yet, God is glorified only as we have a consecrated ministry supported by the labors of a loyal devoted membership. The loss of the Locust Street Greencastle church the first year of the quadrennium reduced the strength of the district. Despite that loss, the following items indicate health and growth.

A stronger ministry is indicated in the fact that four years ago 41% of the pastors in charge were members of conference as against 74% now. Training and preparation in these and the supply pastors show a corresponding increase. In appreciation the pastors' cash support has been increased $7,775.00. Four years ago $46,503.00 was contributed to all benevolences, last year $48,182.00. During the quadrennium $245,510.00 have been paid for new buildings, improvements and debts. The new churches are at Erie; Bloomfield; Fairview, Bloomington; Switz City; and Nashville. There are new parsonages at Bloomfield, Fairview, Arlington, Worthington, and Oolitic.

Indiana University, under the leadership of its great president, is a big factor in the life of the district. Nearly 1200 Methodist students are in attendance. To keep in touch with these for Methodism our Wesley Foundation is doing a splendid work. Our district motto has been "Let Us Be Methodists." This has been a constant inspiration in the attempt to measure up to the full working plan of God and the church. While we have fallen far short of these high ideals, Christ dwelling within gives hope of some day attaining to the perfect life.

CONNERSVILLE DISTRICT, INDIANA CONFERENCE

By John T. Scull, D.D., Superintendent.

Connersville District lies east of Indianapolis and borders the National Road on the south. It is comprised of Shelby, Decatur, Rush, Union, Fayette and Franklin counties. Being a compact territory, every point of the district is easily reached from the head of the district, which is Rushville. Here a commodious district parsonage is provided for the superintendent. The district has thirty-six charges.

During the last four years an effort has been made by the district superintendent to provide these churches with pastors who would serve a sufficient length of time to put on a worth-while program in each charge. He has only partially succeeded. One man has been nine years in his charge, another eight years, six four years, and eight three years. We cannot hope to build the right kind of life into our churches in this day if the itinerant character of our ministry is over-emphasized.

Cultivation programs have characterized the work of the district during the quadrennium. Church music, stewardship, brotherhood work, religious education and World Service have been the themes of these programs.

The outstanding building projects have been: Educational

plant at Brookville, $40,000; church at Greensburg, $165,000; Rushville social and educational addition, $40,000; St. Paul, church, $10,000; Trinity, Shelbyville, church, $45,000; Carthage, parsonage, $3,000; Clarksburg, parsonage, $2,500; Greensburg, parsonage, $12,000; Manilla, parsonage, $3,300; Trinity, Shelbyville, parsonage, $5,000; Waldron, parsonage, $7,000, a total of $333,800. There has been a net increase in property value of $254,443.

A net advance in membership of 1,667 is noted. Ministerial support has increased $5,304. While there has been a decrease of over $9,000 from the World Service givings of 1924, it is encouraging to note that the shrinkage of last year over the previous year was very slight, giving us some degree of assurance that better things may be expected in the years to come. The total benevolent giving for 1927 was $74,546.

Increased emphasis is being laid on evangelism. This is especially noticeable in the current year. The indications are that this will far exceed any other year in evangelistic results.

Seven ministers in the retired relation reside within the bounds of the district. The Rev. J. B. Lathrop, D.D., who is the next oldest minister in Methodism lives at Greensburg. Last November he passed his 102nd year. He is marvelously preserved in body and mind. All of these brethren are a source of great inspiration and help in the district work.

EVANSVILLE DISTRICT, INDIANA CONFERENCE

By George H. Murphy, D.D., Superintendent.

Our forty-eight charges, with their ninety-four churches, cover eight counties in some of the richest and in some of the poorest of our conference territory. Let us take a look at the more favored part first.

Marked advance has come during the quadrennium in the building of seventeen new churches and five parsonages, costing $595,000. Of this, $352,000 has been paid, which, together with payment of the 1924 debt of $17,000 makes a financial achievement of $369,000. The present debt of $243,000 is so heavy as to hinder the normal life of the church. The annual interest of $14,000 is more than our World Service record for any year, and is about twenty per cent of the pastors' cash salary. It depresses the spiritual life also. However, with one possible exception, we shall win out. We have had some splendid revivals with old time altar fire. Our last World Service report turned the tide of slump with a slight increase, for the first time since 1920. In the four years, the pastors' salaries have made a net advance of nine per cent, with payment becoming more prompt. Settlement Day, December 31, 1927, showed only $1100 unpaid of a claim of $18,000 for the first quarter.

The difficult part of our work lies in the remote places, hard of access, especially among the river hills far to the east. Many abandoned Methodist churches tell us what is about to happen to many others barely drawing breath. It seems more difficult every year to meet the meager ministerial support; the reason often given—farm conditions—does not explain. .Our people have what they want most. In a few instances a happy choice of pastors has turned the tide, and the dead has come to life. But the problem is to find worth-while men who will live contentedly in primitive conditions. On a recent visit to the "far east" the superintendent made the last ten miles on foot, and the next morning, after the hill trail had put the buggy out of commission, he made the last six miles out to the State highway astride a horse bareback. After a five hour journey, he came into town singing "Home, Sweet Home" in his heart. Too often the first question with us preachers is "When can I get out of here?" The only future for our work in these places is more adequate support, and to find for each place a real man who will call it "home."

INDIANAPOLIS DISTRICT, INDIANA CONFERENCE

By Orien W. Fifer, D.D., Superintendent

The Indianapolis District is one peculiarly located and constituted for diversified and striking forms of Methodist service in Christ's Kingdom. It is situated in the heart of the Area and its center is the capital city of Indiana. The human field is within a population of over 400,000. This population is largely urban, with industrial, manufacturing and commercial employment prevailing. Agricultural territory, however, is within the district and is among the most productive in the United States. Thriving towns and suburbs surround the city.

The district contains 68 church buildings and 53 pastoral charges. Among these are some unique circuits, several truly metropolitan churches in size, program and membership, and a large number of vigorous churches, from 500 to 1,000 in membership.

The total membership of the district is 26,249 not including 2,538 non-resident-inactive members. This is a gain of 2,655 for the quadrennium. In that period 6,469 persons have been received as preparatory members. These figures do not include the membership of eleven other churches within the district boundaries belonging to the Northwest Indiana, the Lexington and the Central German conferences.

The total of disciplinary and conference benevolences during the quadrennium was $517,779. From 1924 every year marked an increase in the amount contributed for conference benevolences.

The Sunday schools number sixty-five and have an enrollment of 21,130. A district association of Methodist superintendents has been formed.

The Epworth Leagues number 48 with a membership of over 2,000. Six leagues have been organized or reorganized during the past six months. The notable Epworth League enterprise in the district is the Winter Institute held in February every year with an enrollment at the last session of 713. The Junior League membership is 725.

Pastoral support has increased $11,056 during the quadrennium.

The City Council and Church Extension Society organized a few years ago is active and helpful. It is now planning to erect a community building adjoining historic Fletcher Place Church and to house the present Methodist Settlement there with a more extensive program. During the quadrennium the Council aided weak churches; secured the site for and launched the new Fifty-first Street Church; aided the Robindale and Speedway enterprises; bought the lots for Forest Manor Church; helped School Street Church in equipment and remodeling; repaired the buildings of the Methodist Settlement; and rendered great service to Fletcher Place Church in improvements and repairs.

The quadrennium has been notable for church building and improvements. Roberts Park Church has added a new structure costing $110,000. Fountain Street, Blaine Avenue, Castleton, Garfield Avenue, Fifty-first Street, Maywood and Beech Grove have new church buildings. North Church has raised an additional $100,000, and this summer will complete the basement and erect the superstructure of the auditorium. This new enterprise now has assets of over a quarter million dollars and ultimately will mean an expenditure of more than $500,000. West Michigan Street will complete its education building this year. Capitol Avenue built an additional unit for religious and recreational programs. Irvington has completed a plant valued at $300,000. Broadway in October dedicated the main auditorium and transepts representing to date a valuation of $542,000. Additional units when completed will mean a church plant valued at $700,000.

The amount of money expended during the quadrennium for new buildings and improvements was $900,000. The amount paid on old debts was $255,000. The present valuation of church and parsonage property is $3,032,775, an increase for the quadrennium of $1,218,456.

NEW ALBANY DISTRICT, INDIANA CONFERENCE
By J. Edward Murr, D.D., Superintendent.

Indiana Methodism took its rise within the present boundaries of the New Albany District, which includes Floyd, Clark, Scott, Orange, Washington, Crawford, and Harrison Counties. There are forty-three charges, with as many pastors, and 120 churches. Methodism here has maintained much of the old time spirit and power characterizing the Fathers. Without an exception every church in the entire district aims and expects altar conversions during the annual evangelistic campaigns. One marked result is noticeable aside from the salvation of the lost—namely the gaining of many recruits for the ministry. The seven counties comprising this district, together with twenty other counties found in that section of the state immediately south of a line running from Vincennes to North Vernon—all of which is south of the Baltimore and Southwestern Railway—furnish 51% of the ministers of the ninety-two counties of the state; and the same counties furnish 53% of the school teachers of the entire state.

During the quadrennium now closing, $245,000 has been raised and expended in some eight building enterprises. Wall Street Church, Jeffersonville, is now one of the best equipped buildings of the entire conference. The Sunday school addition has made possible a model organization, insured the best of leadership, and has resulted in becoming a real inspiration and example throughout the entire district.

Perhaps the most outstanding single evidence of all around progress during these four years was the work accomplished at Sellersburg. Eight years since the people of that place were worshipping in a small frame building, paying their pastor a cash salary of $600, and requiring him to live in a parsonage that was only such in name. The same membership, with but few exceptions, now worships in a new brick church, their pastor lives in a splendid new parsonage modern in every way, and receives a salary of $2,000.

Aside from the city of New Albany there is no other city numbering 25,000 inhabitants. The marked tendency to the congested centers leaves its inroads. Notwithstanding this constant drainage the four years show a net gain in membership of 1600. In the main our membership is dependent upon the farms for its support, and this through a period of great depression, yet there has been some slight but steady increase in benevolences, and the pastors' salaries during this same period shows a gain of $7000. The average salary of the district is $1450.

The whole of the territory comprising this district is viewed by the state as missionary territory in the matter of education, since every county receives state support in maintaining a school period commensurate with other sections of the state. The church thus far has not been enabled to match the state in maintenance contribution. Both the state and church have a just pride in the many contributions these seven counties have made to the country and Kingdom in the character of the men and women who have gone out from this district. With but few exceptions the citizenship of these counties is descended from the original American parent stock, thus enabling the church to carry forward its program with but slight hinderance beyond the matter of comparative poverty.

SEYMOUR DISTRICT, INDIANA CONFERENCE
By L. C. Jeffrey, D.D., Superintendent.

The Seymour District is located in the heart of the beauty spot of Indiana. It comprises the following counties, Bartholomew, Jackson, Jennings, Ripley, Switzerland, Jefferson, Ohio, and Dearborn. With the beautiful Ohio River skirting the south, the graceful hills of Switzerland County on the southeast, and the bewitching scenery around Madison, one can see nature at its best, with the handiwork of God above his head, and about his feet. If one admires beautiful things, they are all here in this part of the state.

There are forty-two charges, and one hundred and twenty-five churches in the district. Some adjustments have been made. Grace Church, Madison, was merged with Trinity, and this has proved a blessing to both, for now we have a strong church, and Methodism is in the forefront in this thriving city.

Vevay and Moorefield, two small stations, were united into one pastoral charge, and now render more efficient service, the pastor preaching at one church in the morning, and the other at night. Other adjustments can be made, which will increase our efficiency as a church in the district.

First Church, Columbus, has sold the old parsonage, purchased a new site, and erected a modern parsonage at a cost of ten thousand dollars. Seymour remodeled the old church building and added a Sunday school plant, all costing fifty thousand dollars.

Other churches have been erected and improved over the district in various places, adding to our equipment and efficiency.

Many of our rural churches are active and growing, with splendid crowds at every service, good Sunday schools, and live Epworth Leagues. In some localities we are overchurched, even with our own denomination. With the improved roads and automobiles, we could render better service, and reduce expenses if some of our outlying churches would close their doors, come to the center, and unite with other churches of the charge. But alas! it is easy to see what should be done, but another thing to bring it to pass. Sentiment clusters around the old church yard, and it is difficult to persuade one to abandon an old friend; but we must yield in many localities, if we keep step with the times and do the work we are called to do.

Despite the fact that our territory is largely rural and much of the land is poor, we are not only holding our own, but steadily advancing all along the line.

Last year our net gain in church membership was 210, in Sunday school enrollment 370, and Epworth League members 204. The missionary societies are wide awake, and a mighty challenge to the church to follow them to victory in spreading the gospel message to the unchurched of America and the heathen lands.

Our people believe in the Methodist Church, are willing to support its program, are loyal to its doctrines, and believe in the power of Christ to save from sin and keep in the way of eternal life. We are not discouraged. We are not satisfied with past achievements, but we have a will to work and a faith in God that will not be denied, and we will carry on until Christ is crowned king in every heart, or we are called to join the ranks of those who have washed their robes and made them white in the blood of the lamb.

"We'll work till Jesus comes,
And then be gathered home."

THE VINCENNES DISTRICT, INDIANA CONFERENCE

By R. H. Toole, D.D., Superintendent.

Within the past quadrennium there has been a net gain in membership of 691, making the present total membership 16,848. The total Sunday school enrollment is 16,459, with an average attendance of 8,756. The total Epworth League membership, including both junior and senior members is 2,053.

In ministerial support there has been a net gain of $5,052.00; the total support last conference year being $79,911.00.

The total contributed to World Service during the quadrennium was $43,230.00. The Woman's Foreign Missionary Society paid a total to missions of $25,928.00, and the Womans' Home Missionary Society contributed $7,723.00. The grand total of all benevolences for the quadrennium amounts to $205,740.00.

The following church buildings have been constructed or completed: Winslow, costing approximately $31,000; Alford, $2,500; Wheatland, $17,000; on the Pimento Charge, $7,000; and the Sullivan Sunday school annex, $40,000.

Vincennes North church has erected a new parsonage at a cost of $3,000.00.

A new church with provision for Sunday school and social life is in process of construction at Decker, to be completed this conference year.

The total expended for buildings, improvements, and indebtedness during the quadrennium was $172,920.00.

The Western Christian Advocate subscriptions at last conference report was 1,272, being a gain of 202 during the quadrennium.

GREENSBURG

MADISON, MUNCIE

BEECH GROVE

IRVINGTON

BROADWAY, INDIANAPOLIS

FIRST, GARY

ST. MARK'S GOSHEN

WAYNEDALE CHURCH
FT. WAYNE

HARTFORD CITY

SOME NEW CHURCHES

FORT WAYNE DISTRICT, NORTH INDIANA CONFERENCE

By Warren W. Wiant, D.D., Superintendent.

Fort Wayne District in Methodist geography covers Steuben, most of Dekalb, Allen, Adams and Wells Counties. It reaches one hundred miles from north to south, and from twenty to forty miles east and west. With the city of Fort Wayne as the center, this district is most favorably situated with thriving manufacturing interests in all of the larger towns, and it covers some of the finest agricultural land in Indiana.

In its relationship to North Indiana Conference and to the church in general, the district has an enviable record. This year First Church, Fort Wayne, celebrates her first one hundred years of history, a period beginning with the organization of Methodism in northeastern Indiana.

The church is now passing through a period of transition in this section. With the coming of better roads, the consolidation of the public schools, and the general use of the automobile, many of our rural churches that were active and influential a few years ago are closing their doors. We are coming to a time when we shall have fewer and better equipped church buildings, with the statistics showing a steady advance in membership. Methodism is proving her adaptability by splendidly meeting the new conditions in many parts of the district.

In the city of Fort Wayne our church is keeping step with a rapidly growing population. Forest Park Church, located in a lovely residential section, northeast, has passed its first five years of history and is on the eve of a campaign for a permanent building. Waynedale Church is nearing completion, at a cost of $32,000, and will serve a population of three thousand people where was open country six or seven years ago. St. Paul's Church has sold its location and will erect a new building this coming year on a site already purchased, nearly a mile east and north of the present church home. The Methodist Hospital, located in the very heart of the city, is making an ever increasing number of friends each year with its efficient ministries of mercy and healing.

The Woman's Home Missionary Society of North Indiana Conference, has erected a Neighborhood House at John and Horace Streets in Fort Wayne, where a seven day per week program is conducted among the foreign born peoples and their children, with far-reaching results.

The Epworth Leagues of the district lead all the districts in the church in money given for missions and in booth festivals which they conduct annually. They hold the Area banner given by Bishop Leonard for the highest rank in Methodism for work done during his leadership as president of the Board of Epworth League.

Last year, 1926-1927, this district led its conference in giving for World Service and gains in the church membership. All the various activities of the church flourish in this territory. Methodism in Fort Wayne District is "onward bound" to a still greater day with the passing of the years.

GOSHEN DISTRICT, NORTH INDIANA CONFERENCE

By Charles H. Smith, D.D., Superintendent.

The Goshen District of the North Indiana Conference has made some real progress in the past four years. The Conference Minutes of 1924 showed the membership in full connection to be 14,169 while the Minutes of 1927 record a membership in full connection of 15,107.

While the benevolences suffered the usual post-Centenary slump the downward trend was stopped last year and a gain registered. The auxiliaries of both the Woman's Home and Foreign Missionary Societies have shown steady gains each year until they lead the districts of the North Indiana Conference.

One of the notable advances of the district within the quadrennium has been in the matter of church and parsonage building and improvement. New buildings have been erected at Simpson, Elkhart, and East Mishawaka. St. Mark's, Goshen, Atwood and Helmer have been reconstructed so thoroughly that they are like new buildings. Trinity, Elkhart, First Church, Goshen, and Osceola have completed splendid new church school annexes which make them thoroughly modern. Wakarusa and Milford have erected thoroughly modern parsonage buildings, while the South Milford parsonage has been rebuilt and modernized. Troublesome debts have been entirely paid or greatly reduced at Milford, Butler, Scott, Kendallville, Leesburg, Pierceton, and Warsaw. Extensive improvements have been made on the church or parsonage property at the following places: Albion, Avilla, Bourbon, Tippecanoe, Butler, Wayne Center, Inwood, Cromwell, Wolf Lake, LaGrange, Leesburg, Ligonier, First Church, Mishawaka, New Paris, Benton, Pierceton, South Milford, Syracuse, Topeka, Wakarusa, Waterloo, Wawaka and Wolcottville.

Religious education has received due consideration in the program of the district. Not only is an effort made to bring the church schools of the district up to a high order, but daily vacation Bible schools have been fostered until all but nine of the pastoral charges have some form of daily religious instruction among the children of grade school age.

Without exception the various conventions and conferences of the district have been well attended both by laymen and ministers. The morale of the district is maintained at a high level and the prospects are good for an advance in every line of activity.

LOGANSPORT DISTRICT, NORTH INDIANA CONFERENCE

By L. C. Bentley, D.D., Superintendent.

Logansport District lies in the central part of the State. It covers Tipton, Howard, and Miami counties, and parts of Hamilton, Clinton, and Cass. Its land is well adapted to agriculture and stock raising.

There are forty-seven pastoral charges, having seventy-three churches, forty-six parsonages and holding seventy-three Sunday schools. These schools have an enrollment of 15,552, with an average attendance of 55% which is a gain for the quadrennium of seven percent.

During these years the statistics show there has been expended in ministerial support $410,338. There has been paid on current expenses $215,785. The people have expended for building and improvements $198,635, and they have given for benevolences at home and abroad $287,875. This makes a total of $1,107,-606. It is an annual expenditure of $16.00 per member.

Church buildings have been improved in fifteen charges. New churches have been built at Lincoln, Cassville, Chili, South Side Elwood, and two in Kokomo—Parr Memorial and Trinity. The last two churches were made possible through the Kokomo Methodist Social Union which was organized three years ago.

Earnest effort has been made to strengthen the churches in life and membership. Young people in junior and senior Leagues have been trained in special courses. About 300 have attended institute each year. Daily vacation Bible schools have increased annually. Church night schools are held. One of the largest in the area is held at Peru. It has a weekly attendance of over 250.

Every approved mode of evangelism has been practiced. No church has passed a year without an evangelistic meeting. Most of these meetings are held by the pastors. Many people have come into the churches. But owing to over-much correcting of the roll, little gain is shown.

The work of the women has been encouraging. There are twenty-eight auxiliaries of the Foreign Missionary Society. They have contributed $23,817. The twenty Home Societies have raised $19,487. There are sixty-eight Ladies' Aid Societies which have made $104,486. The total raised by these women is $147,-690. This is better than the church has done. It has suffered a reduction. These women teach the church the need of a more careful training in stewardship and a wider distribution of responsibility.

There have been two financial campaigns in the district. The first was an effort to raise $100,000 for the Preachers' Aid Society. The second was for the Methodist hospitals of the State. Both efforts were successful.

All church indebtedness reported on the district at the beginning of the quadrennium, except in the case of three churches has been paid. But other indebtedness has been incurred. The total is about the same.

During the years reported no church has been abandoned and

no society discontinued. Three churches have been organized, with Sunday schools. They represent an expenditure of $28,000; current expenses of $3,000; benevolences of $510; a Sunday school enrollment of 375; and a church membership of 250.

MUNCIE DISTRICT, NORTH INDIANA CONFERENCE

By William T. Arnold, D.D., District Superintendent.

Muncie District comprises all of Delaware, Madison, Hamilton, and parts of Blackford and Grant Counties, with headquarters in the city of Muncie. The district has at present forty-one charges with as many pastors. There are at present sixty-eight church buildings and thirty-nine parsonages. The story of material and spiritual growth within this progressive district for the past quadrennium has been a joy and delight to both pastors and laymen. The work reflects great credit upon our worthy and energetic pastors. Eight new churches have been built during the past four years at a cost of $304,000. They are: Fairview on the Albany circuit, Beach Grove on the Alexandria Circuit, Grace Church, Anderson, Mt. Pleasant on the DeSoto Circuit, Eaton, Madison Street, Muncie, Shideler, and Grace Church, Hartford City. Two new structures at High Street and Normal City are to be erected soon at a cost of $377,245.

There has been a steady advance in ministerial support. Pastors' salaries made a total gain of $9,600. The district superintendent's salary has been increased $1,200. The campaign for the Methodist Hospital in this district during the past four years netted a subscription of $46,000, and for the DePauw-Greencastle Church, $10,000.

The Woman's Foreign Missionary Society has raised $47,942, and the Woman's Home Missionary Society about $20,539.

The district has been faithful to the World Service program, having raised $162,516.

The spiritual advancement has kept pace with the material progress. The ministers of the district believe that Methodism was born in a revival: that in the providence of God it has furnished the inspiration for the great awakening in individual Christians and the church. Pastors have shouldered the responsibility in their churches, and consecrated laymen have joined them. As a result there have been thousands of conversions and reclamations. During the quadrennium there have been 7,304 accessions to the membership, a net gain in membership of 1,047. About 1,300 have been baptized, and over 3,000 received into preparatory membership.

The Sunday schools are all prosperous and report an increasing average attendance. There are thirty-two Epworth Leagues doing excellent work and sending 298 young people to Epworth Forest Institute.

Every phase of district work has made progress. The gains have not all been as large as might be hoped, but have been steady, consistent, and evenly balanced. Muncie District has always stood, and now stands solidly behind the program of the Methodist Episcopal Church, and it will continue to do so.

RICHMOND DISTRICT, NORTH INDIANA CONFERENCE

By Fred F. Thornburg, D.D., Superintendent.

Richmond District comprises forty-five charges. Of these, twenty-three are stations, fourteen are two-point, and eight are three-point works, while two churches have irregular services. Four churches are in towns of seventeen thousand population and above, twelve in towns ranging from one thousand to six thousand souls, forty-five in villages and hamlets and sixteen are out in the open country. The district covers five counties, Hancock, Henry, Wayne, Randolph and Jay, together with small portions of Madison and Blackford.

In common with most districts World Service suffered severe losses the first half of the quadrennium, but the third year stemmed the downward current with $796 to the good, and this year promises to recover us still further.

A sad story is the apparent slump in membership, but literally hundreds could not be found, even on the records, and others were lost by means of the inactive lists made legal by the last General Conference. The first year of this period Dr. Somerville Light was superintendent.

Minister's cash salaries have increased since last General Conference from $74,800 to $77,950, or 4.2%. The support of conference claimants has increased from $7,211 to $8,476, or 17.5%.

The second year of this period was made historic by the merging of First and Grace churches in Richmond, and the resulting Central Church has a most wonderful opportunity for service. Subscriptions totaling $150,000 have been secured for a new church. The two old properties are still in possession of the trustees.

Eighteen young men have entered the ministry in this district this quadrennium, four of whom have since entered other callings, two are in doubt, one is in school while others are planning to go. Twelve of the eighteen are making good in a fine way.

The chapters of the Epworth League within this district have helped materially in making Epworth Forest Institute the greatest in Methodism, and propose this year to erect, as their gift to the Institute, an administration building, housing the book store, the post office, the registration and directors' rooms. The basement will be used for assembly and recitations.

Many individual societies and outstanding achievements should have special mention, but space forbids. The spirit of the district urges on to the attempt of greater things in the next four years.

WABASH DISTRICT, NORTH INDIANA CONFERENCE

By U.S.A. Bridge, D.D., Superintendent.

"Advance" has been the aim of the Wabash District this quadrennium, and advance there has been.

The District Epworth League was organized in September, 1889. In the past three years it has made great progress. In District convention it has reached an attendance of 1000, and in enrollment in the Epworth Forest Institute it has registered as high as 633. It has taken a long stride in attendance and offering at the Booth Festival and has undertaken to provide the support of a missionary.

In an attempt at the solution of the rural church problem several churches were merged and a church built at the center of the township where the consolidated township school is located. There is now a flourishing church where otherwise there would soon have been a large community without a church.

A plan for securing a district parsonage has been adopted by the District stewards and the District conference. Though the process of gathering funds has been under way only a few months several thousand dollars are in the treasury.

A district paper has been published. Though small, and issued quarterly, it has been the means of carrying the message through the mail to all the pastors and all members of the Quarterly conferences. This paper, with other publicity and extensive speaking campaigns, have carried the interests of the Kingdom to all the churches in the district.

The improvement of church property has kept pace with needs, at an outlay of $78,943. Indebtedness has been reduced. Pastors' salaries have been advanced, though some are not sufficient to provide an adequate support. In giving to the benevolences the movement is in the right direction.

The real work of the church in building Christian character and in saving life has been faithfully prosecuted. There have been a number of gracious revivals in the district, through which there has come added strength to the church.

Within the district is our Home for the Aged. Here lives a large company of happy men and women. Four colleges are located in the district, all of which are ministering in a large way to many young people.

CRAWFORDSVILLE DISTRICT, NORTHWEST INDIANA CONFERENCE.

By Otto Tevis Martin, D.D., Superintendent.

The Crawfordsville District covers an excellent agricultural section of Indiana, and therefore would be classed as a rural district. Our membership being largely from the country, we have had some grave economic problems to overcome during the last three years. Because of this, and owing to the fact that our churches are in old and well established communities, we have not made a rapid gain, but through the loyalty and devotion of the pastors and people, we have made some gain in all the departments of the church activities.

During the last three years our pastors have made a careful survey of the communities, and by personal endeavor we have been able, in some degree, to overcome the habit of church members moving into communities without taking fellowship in the churches in that community. Laying stress on this and the evangelistic programs of our church, we have brought into the fellowship of our churches 4,266 members, this being fully one-third of the total membership at the beginning of the quadrennium. However, because of the misunderstanding concerning the reporting of non-resident and inactive members, the full membership of our church now registers only a ten percent gain, though there has been a large gain in the non-resident and inactive list.

The laity have shown their interest in the local finance of the church and the properties by making special sacrifices in order to keep many of our churches moving forward. We have built two new churches and practically rebuilt a third, making a total gain in the valuation of our church properties of over two hundred thousand dollars, and during the same period have reduced our church indebtedness thirty-one thousand dollars. Also, in many places, chiefly in the small towns where the living support of our pastors was below standard, we have increased the pastoral support over ten thousand dollars and every charge has reported all pastoral claims paid in full at the close of each conference year.

The work among our young people has not been outstanding, but we have made gains in the number of chapters in our Epworth League and also a small gain in membership. The enrollment of Sunday schools remained about the same.

Following the fearful reaction after the Centenary period, the offering for World Service in this district fell from $33,449.00 to $14,650.00. We have been able to stop the decline and to rally our churches to this great cause. Three years ago less than thirty percent of our membership was giving to the World Service. Last year fifty percent of our membership supported this cause, and we have made a gain of ten percent in the offering and are encouraged to feel that we shall continue on the ascending scale.

We have not accomplished all we would have wished, but feel through His blessing and the splendid cooperation of pastors and people that we have made headway. We face the future with greater faith and stronger heart, sure of victory in His name.

GREENCASTLE DISTRICT, NORTHWEST INDIANA CONFERENCE

By A. T. Briggs, D.D., Superintendent.

The Greencastle District is served by fifty-one pastors. Twenty-eight are resident, ten are local, and thirteen are students. Half of the charges are small in numbers and in material resources. Yet the district makes a creditable showing in the items tabulated in the conference minutes.

One hundred and ninety thousand dollars have been spent in the construction of three new churches and in the improvement of fourteen others. Plans have been made for the building of three new churches in the near future, one at Montrose, Terre Haute; one at Riverside Park, Indianapolis; and the other at Greencastle, which will require $375,000 for their completion.

The most outstanding need of the district is the Greencastle church. The hearty and unqualified endorsement by the joint committee of DePauw trustees, the commission from the Area Council, and trustees of the local church insures the completion of this great enterprise.

World Service shows a slight decrease in offerings. When the financial depression due to strikes, floods, and unemployment throughout the district is taken into account, the wonder is that the district has done so well.

The membership shows a slight increase annually. It stands at 17,000. The spirit of evangelism is in evidence and shows itself through mass meetings and visitation campaigns. The goal of the district has been a net increase of ten percent in membership. A number of churches have exceeded this low percentage.

The Sunday schools show a steady advance in membership and efficiency. Special stress has been placed upon the care and nurture of the youth. The Junior Church, the Epworth League, and organized classes are making fine contributions to that end. Both the Woman's Home and Foreign Missionary Societies have made a commendable advance each year.

The district is loyal to the entire program of the Methodist Episcopal Church and to the policies of the Indianapolis Area. It is glad to have a small part in putting the Area among the first of the whole church.

LAFAYETTE DISTRICT, NORTHWEST INDIANA CONFERENCE.

By John J. Wilson, D.D., Superintendent.

The Lafayette District is in the "corn belt" of Indiana, and is typically rural. Lafayette is the only city within its bounds. Of the sixty-eight churches of the district eight are located in county seat towns, forty-one in rural towns and villages, and thirteen in the open country. The district includes the whole of five counties and parts of four others. Its shape is irregularly fan-like, radiating west, north, and northeast from Lafayette. Twenty-four charges of the district are stations, the remainder are two or three-point circuits.

The property valuation of the district, including only churches and parsonages, totals $775,000. During the quadrennium nine new churches have been built new, ten have been repaired and rebuilt, and three new parsonages completed. Of the sixty-eight church organizations all but one hold their service in buildings owned by the church.

The total benevolent giving of the district has averaged $68,-211 annually for the quadrennium. The average annual total for World Service for the quadrennium has been $19,137. The total membership is 15,048, and each year of the quadrennium has witnessed a slight gain.

Three of the Northwest Indiana Conference institutions are within the boundary of the district: the Battle Ground Assembly, the Monnett School for Girls at Rensselaer, and The Wesley Foundation at Purdue.

The Battle Ground Assembly, comprising eighty acres of land with a tabernacle, a modern up to date hotel, fifty-six cottages and other conveniences for service is the seat of the School of Missions fostered by the Women's Home and the Woman's Foreign Missionary Societies of the conference, the Epworth League Institute where upward of eight hundred young people gather one week each year for training and inspiration, a Sunday School Training Conference where more than two hundred and fifty workers meet for a week, and the Bible Conference where study classes, pastors conferences, and forums with intensive evangelistic meetings are held each year.

The Monnett School for girls is a boarding school for girls where thirty-five to forty girls, some orphans, others children of broken homes, and some children of parents whose occupations make home life and training impossible, are educated and given Christian training. Splendidly trained, self sacrificing teachers make possible to these young people service of a type and degree found in but few institutions.

The Wesley Foundation at Purdue, with a separate plant and equipment under the direction of the Rev. M. C. Hunt, pastor of the First Church of West Lafayette and the associate pastor and student leader, the Rev. H. D. Bollinger, does a type of work for the Methodist students of Purdue University outstanding in its appeal and challenge. More than thirteen hundred Methodist students gather each year at Purdue for scholastic training. The Foundation with its sociability and Christian educational emphasis provides a home and help for them. The results are evident in the definite loyalty of the students and their unqualified tribute to the timely Christian service rendered.

SOUTH BEND DISTRICT, NORTHWEST INDIANA CONFERENCE

By B. D. Beck, D.D., Superintendent.

Growth is a marked characteristic of this section of the state. Fourteen trunk lines of railways, together with Lake Michigan, make transportation easy. This is destined to be the greatest industrial center in the world. Around these industries cities are growing. Contributary industries push out into smaller cities and give them new life.

All this is a mighty challenge to the church. In spite of our efforts to keep the church in the forefront of this progress it often seems that industrial life is outrunning religion. However, some of our people are no longer content to see industries that involve millions of money and tens of thousands of men rise up around them while they offer unto the Lord that which costs them nothing. Consequently we are building some churches that are symbolic of the values of religion and that are adequate to make religion's contribution to society.

Including two new churches in process of construction we have added to and built new churches and parsonages this quadrennium to the value of $1,356,000. The current expense item has grown from $69,505 to $101,089. Counting salaries being paid the pastors this year, together with parsonage rent, there has been a gain of $12,605. As a rule the dollars of the church do not increase when the spiritual interest is at a standstill or declines.

For benevolences figures speak for themselves. In 1924 the district gave to the Centenary $34,836. The three years since it has given $32,401, $34,286 and $34,653 respectively. We own with shame the lack of growth there. We get a bit of comfort out of the fact that most others have done worse. At the same time we raised our giving to annual conference benevolences from $6,766 in 1924 to $19,699, $19,857 and $21,670 for the three years following. Thus our giving to others has increased $13,000 per year.

We started the quadrennium with 18,184 active members. We received from preparatory membership and on confession of faith 2,956 in the three years, and by certificate 2,588, making a total of 5,544. But our 1927 minutes show 18,981 active members which is a gain of only 797. In this time we have lost 562 members by death. Consequently we have lost 4,185 members by transfer out and to the non-resident and inactive roll. A special campaign is now on to reach as many as possible of this number. While the Sunday schools generally have lost in their enrollment the last four years we are happy to report a gain of 559. The Epworth Leagues were never better.

Religious education in week-day schools has its serious difficulties, not the least financial support. But it is fixing its roots more firmly every year in this territory. The women's organizations all grow, while new interest is awakened in men's work.

CARBONDALE DISTRICT, SOUTHERN ILLINOIS CONFERENCE.

By W. M. Brown, D.D., Superintendent.

The Carbondale District, Southern Illinois Conference, is the southernmost district in Illinois and covers twelve of the one hundred counties. Much of this is hill country only recently developing value as a remarkable orchard section. The chief other industry is coal mining, which creates its own problems. Scattered through its five thousand miles are a dozen considerable cities, and numerous smaller towns. Rural work in a distinctive sense is lacking.

In this territory the Methodist Episcopal Church has forty-three charges, and one conference institution—Holden Hospital. To this work are appointed thirty-eight conference men and five supplies. These are paid a total of $76,614.00, an average of $1,760. Twenty-six appointments are stations, four two-point, and thirteen circuits. This work on the whole is well housed; sixteen churches being recently remodeled. Every appointment possesses a parsonage property, and a number of these compare favorably with any house in their communities. The total property value is upward of one million dollars with an outstanding indebtedness of only seven percent. Of these values one hundred and seventy-five thousand dollars were paid during the quadrennium.

Using these properties are 12,273 members, distributed among eighty churches; the largest of these has a membership of eight hundred; half a dozen churches are approximately of this size. Eighty Sunday schools have a membership of 14,257 and an average attendance of 7,851. A considerable number of the charges are hindered during much of the year by heavy roads, but remarkable changes are following the extensive building of hard roads.

The district has shown a deep interest in evangelism. Meetings are held annually on practically every charge. (These are in great favor with the people.) About four hundred weeks of meetings have been held during the quadrennium. The net gain in membership is one thousand.

During this period the district has given for all benevolences a total of $81,985. This is distributed in three approximately equal groups—$21,584 for World Service; $23,250 for other disciplinary benevolences and $37,151 for conference interests. Of these conference interests, Holden hospital, located at Carbondale, Illinois, is closest to us. Its plant is valued at $175,000. It has a hospital staff of seventeen persons, including twelve nurses in training. Its first commencement for training school occurs in June 1928, when six nurses receive diplomas, and are eligible for the R. N. examinations. The hospital has had a remarkable record for efficiency, and low death rate. It has fifty beds and is fully accredited.

CENTRALIA DISTRICT, SOUTHERN ILLINOIS CONFERENCE

By C. B. Whiteside, D.D., Superintendent.

Centralia District, composed of 45 charges and 105 churches, is located in the north central part of the Southern Illinois Conference. It represents one of the 24 denominations serving this section of Illinois. Of the 414 churches thus located 105 are Methodist Episcopal; 68, the next largest number, are Baptist; and 41, the next in order, are Disciples.

Centralia District, and practically the entire conference is rural. Only one town in the district has a population of more than 3500. Only one church in the district pays above $2100 for the support of the pastor. The average salary for the district is $1208. The occupation of the people of this section is farming, fruit growing, dairying, poultry raising, and mining, on a small scale. The land is poor and that effects other industries.

Withal, the value of church and parsonage property stands at $752,075, an increase for the quadrennium of $94,375. There has been an increase during the same time of $10,153 in total ministerial support. The statistics on church membership show an increase for the four years of 1815. In no single year of the four has there been a decrease in membership. Only one year has there been a decrease in Sunday school enrollment. We are giving less

WALL STREET, JEFFERSONVILLE

WESLEY HALL, GOSHEN

WAYNE STREET, FT. WAYNE

TRINITY, EVANSVILLE

ROBERTS PARK, INDIANAPOLIS

CAPITOL AVENUE, INDIANAPOLIS

MODERN COMMUNITY UNITS

by half for World Service than we were giving for the Centenary when we entered the quadrennium. But for all benevolences we are giving more than we did for the same causes when we started in four years ago. When we consider the giving for all purposes there has been a decided increase.

The success of the Kingdom is its greatest embarrassment. The greatest need of this day is grace and wisdom sufficient to bring about co-operation, and, in many instances, union, so that instead of spending our resources in simply maintaining an existence, we may be moving forward as a mighty army.

EAST ST. LOUIS DISTRICT, SOUTHERN ILLINOIS CONFERENCE.

By W. H. Whitlock, D.D., Superintendent.

This district includes the most densely populated section of Illinois outside of Chicago. For twenty years it has been a problematical "new frontier." It has not been possible to build schools and churches fast enough to meet the needs of the growing population.

Twenty years ago there were thirty-eight English and seven German charges. All are now merged, and there are fifty-two charges with 11,052 members. Twenty rural charges with 2,462 members have declined to eighteen charges having 1,961 members. Urban charges have increased from eighteen with a membership of 3,772 to twenty-six, with 8,245 members. A dozen churches have been built and substantial additions made to others within the past ten years. The statistics of the German churches are not in the hands of the writer, so are not included in the comparison.

At World Service rate of distribution the district has paid $63,827 to the Board of Home Missions and Church Extension in the past eight years. It has received back into its own work $46,672. That is splendid consideration and much appreciated. This has been used almost entirely to meet the pioneer needs of these American communities.

Some of the largest blocs of Europeans in the central west are within this territory. Only the smallest beginnings have been made in church work among them. The church at the East St. Louis Settlement, at Livingston and at Benld have been made possible by help from the Philadelphia board. In the two latter places we are the only Protestant church in a population of some 6,500, less than ten per cent being American English. With 2,000 in the combined public schools our Sunday schools have only 150. The following communities of the same type do not have a church in them, Jew, Catholic, or Protestant, though there are more than twenty teachers in their public schools: Maryville, Wilsonville, Sawyerville, Edgarville, and No. 3 Mine. The foreign field is not the only one suffering from the slump in World Service.

Will the older, established sections stand by faithfully for a few more years? This work can then not only maintain itself but also be a source of supply for other yet undeveloped fields.

MT. CARMEL DISTRICT, SOUTHERN ILLINOIS CONFERENCE

By C. L. Peterson, D.D., Superintendent.

The Mt. Carmel District covers territorially the major portion of the following nine counties, Jefferson, Wayne, Edwards, Wabash, Franklin, Hamilton, White, Saline, and Galatin.

There are 110 church organizations with a membership of 12,836, grouped into forty-five pastoral charges. These forty-five charges are ministered to by thirty-five members of the annual conference and ten supplies. Besides these pastors there are twenty-two local preachers and twenty exhorters.

The estimated value of the church buildings is $909,800 and of the forty-three parsonages is $137,400. The value of other properties, bonds and endowments is $25,500. The Orphans' and Childrens' Home, a conference institution located at Mt. Vernon, within the bounds of this district, having a capacity for fifty-six children besides the helpers and officers and yearly caring for seventy-five to eighty children who are orphans or dependents, is valued conservatively at $100,000.

The present indebtedness on church property is $147,647. The ninety-seven Sunday schools of the district have enrolled as pupils 14,855. The thirty-two chapters of the senior League have a membership of 1,296. Eight hundred boys and girls are organized and trained in nineteen junior Leagues. The women of the district are organized into sixty-two Ladies Aid societies, which raised and contributed to the church last year $22,800; and into twenty auxiliaries of the W.F.M.S. with 624 members, which raised last year $3,260; and also into nineteen auxiliaries of the W.H.M.S. with 629 members, which contributed to their work last year $3,080.

During the quadrennium now closing this district has raised through the various organizations and paid out through the many channels of the church the following sums of money: to ministerial claims $267,955; to World Service $30,008; to total disciplinary benevolences $58,655; to conference benevolences $38,-190; to church buildings and improvements $202,390; to old indebtedness $68,650; to current expenses $80,699; through the W.F.M.S. $12,473; and through the W.H.M.S. $11,891; a grand total of unrepeated sums of $770,891.

From 1924 to 1928 eight hundred and twenty-three children were baptized; 1,933 adults were baptized; and 2,745 were received into the church on probation and confession.

When these facts are reviewed and the net increase of only 242 members over 1924 is given, some astonishment may rightly be occasioned. But it must be remembered a large portion of the churches are in the rural section and that seventeen charges are dependent on the coal industry for support.

The economic depression in agriculture and also in the coal fields of Southern Illinois for the past four years has caused a general exodus from the farms and the mines to the big industrial cities.

OLNEY DISTRICT, SOUTHERN ILLINOIS CONFERENCE
By Frank O. Wilson, D.D., Superintendent.

Olney District has forty pastoral charges. Eleven churches are in towns, forty-one are in villages, and seventy are in the open country. We do not have a mining or large manufacturing region within our borders. We have some oil and gas wells and a few small factories. This is almost wholly an agricultural district with all the handicaps that the farmer encounters. Here is a wonderful opportunity for men of God who desire to render a great service to their country, to their fellowmen, and to God.

Epworth League study classes, teacher training classes, mid-year institutes, daily vacation Bible schools, and church night schools are on the increase. The League interests are all encouraging and the work is developing a fine group of young people who will take their place in the church somewhere. In districts like this the future large town and city church leaders are now being trained.

The World Service giving has fallen far down the scale but last year the district started up the hill, and unless other interests come in to hinder more increase will be made this year. One church in this district is now paying $3000 to World Service and $2500 to McKendree College.

In the past four years many of the village and country churches have been improved to take care of the interests of the community. We have many hard roads and yet the muddy roads make the greatest hinderance to the year-round active program of the church.

Activities

THE STATE AND AREA COUNCILS.

By C. Howard Taylor, D.D., Secretary.

At the final meeting of the State Council of the Indianapolis Area for the quadrennium, '24-'28, the committee appointed to present plans for the continuation of this organization made the following report:

"We, the committee selected to outline a future course of action for the State Council, submit the following for your consideration:—For nearly eight years under the leadership of our beloved Bishop Frederick DeLand Leete, Indiana Methodism has steadily moved forward and has attained heights undreamed of at the organization of the Indianapolis Area. We have trod the mountain tops of vision and exaltation together. We have journeyed to the Vale of Shadows with our beloved leaders as they passed over to the better land to receive the greetings of our great Elder Brother; we have learned that so far as Indiana Methodism is concerned, "All we are brethren." We recommend first,— that the Indiana State Council of the Methodist Episcopal Church be continued and that a session be held annually in connection with the fall session of the Area Council for the transaction of such business as concerns Indiana Methodism alone. Second, that the delegates to the State and Area Councils be elected by the district conferences as provided in the constitution. Third, that the standing committee of one minister and one layman from each conference be appointed by the Chair annually to nominate officers for the Indiana State Council and to assign the members to their respective committees. Fourth, that the Executive Committee and the standing committees of the State Council shall be and are hereby authorized to carry on the work of the State Council during the interim of its meetings and report their action to the annual meeting of the Council for its approval. Fifth, we recommend that a committee consisting of one minister and one layman from each conference be appointed, which with the

Bishop ex officio shall make a thoughtful survey of our accomplishments in the past four years and a study of what the major objectives of Methodism in Indiana for the next four years should be."

It would be difficult to formulate a better statement of the mission and method of the State Council of Indiana Methodism than is incorporated in this report. The mission of this organization is to unify the work and the workers of the Methodist Episcopal Church in Indiana. That this mission has been performed in a most encouraging way is the universal judgment of the many men and women who have been privileged to share in the endeavor. The method of the organization is to bring together twice yearly elected delegates from all sections of the state and accredited representatives of all the institutions within the state through which Methodism is functioning, for survey and review and council and prayerful consideration of every great interest of the Church related in anywise to this field. The high appreciation of this method of promoting the work of the Church in the state is evidenced in the fact that ministers and laymen are a unit in demanding that the organization shall be continued.

The General Conference of 1924 took away from the Indianapolis Area the Lexington Conference, and gave us instead the Southern Illinois Conference. This change made necessary the organization of an Area Council, in order that our brethren from Illinois might have a share in the benefits of such a council. The first step toward such an organization was taken by the State Council at its meeting in Indianapolis, June 24, 1924. A committee was appointed to devise a plan of organization and to make their report to the State Council at their fall meeting. The following report was made to the State Council at its meeting in Indianapolis, November 5, 1924:

"Your Committee on organization of an Area Council recommends that there be organized an Area Council as provided in the Discipline of our Church; that the Southern Illinois Conference have representation upon the same basis as that upon which the State Council is now made up and share in like manner in area expenses; that the Area Council meet annually in the fall at the call of the Area Office, and that the Indiana State Council have an annual meeting in the spring as heretofore, and that a similar spring meeting be provided for the Southern Illinois Conference. We also recommend that the Bishop and secretary of the Council be authorized to make such changes in the constitution of the State Council as may be necessary to carry this into effect, should those charged with the responsibility of the organization of the Area Council conform to this recommendation."

This report was adopted by the Council and the necessary steps taken to effect the Area organization. The first meeting of the Area Council was held in Terre Haute, October 20, 21, 1926. This was a meeting of great profit, addressed by such outstanding leaders of the Church as Dr. W. S. Bovard, Dr. John R. Edwards, Dr. F. I. Johnson, and Dr. R. J. Wade. The fellowship of these days was delightful, proving that among Methodist preachers state boundaries do not matter much. The session closed with a stirring address by Dr. W. E. J. Gratz.

One of the achievements of the State and Area Councils has been to set up the area goals toward which the churches might strive. Early in the quadrennium the following motto and goals were adopted:—"The motto of this area is 'CHRIST FIRST.' Our goals are,—a minimum net gain in membership for the quadrennium of 15%, every Methodist child adequately trained for Christ and the Church, every member a generous contributor to Christian undertakings at home and abroad, a quickened religious life and thorough religious work in all our communities."

One of the marked achievements of this quadrennium has been the awakening of an historic consciousness among Indiana Methodists. Until recently, the places of historical interest to Methodism in the state have been altogether neglected. Through the State Council a movement was inaugurated to rescue the old Bethel Meeting-house near Charlestown from destruction by the elements, remove it to the town, and provide for its preservation as a Methodist shrine in the Hoosier State. This splendid work was accomplished under the direction of a committee of which J. E. Murr and J. W. Morrow were the directing members. The Indiana Conference, at its 1925 session, held in Jeffersonville, took time off to go to Charlestown in a body and hold a most fitting and inspiring memorial service in and around the old chapel. So great is the historic interest awakened among the preachers of this area through the work of the Council, that preparations are now being made to cooperate with the state commission in the celebration of the one hundred and fiftieth anniversary of the capture of Fort Sackville, which will take place at Vincennes in the near future.

The hospital interests, the educational interests, the care of orphans and aged, all have come under the immediate survey of the Council and have been promoted by it. Early in the quadrennium the great Hospital Advance, under the leadership of Dr. John W. Hancher, was pushed through to a successful issue. While the State Council had no official relation to it, the Council was influential in opening the way for it. As a direct result of this financial achievement, all four of our hospitals in the state are prospering, and the great Methodist Hospital in Indianapolis is engaged in a development which promises to make it the largest and best equipped Methodist hospital in America. Through the work of the State Council it has been possible to bring the two Wesley Foundations of the state at Purdue and Indiana Universities closer together, and to pave the way for an ultimate pooling of all the Wesley Foundation interests in the state, so as to make one common appeal to our Methodist people for this work. This will undoubtedly be in the interest of securing a more adequate support for this most important work, and will reduce the number of appeals for money being made to the churches. During the quadrennium an attempt has been made through the Council to provide the necessary financial help for the building of an adequate church structure in Greencastle to accommodate the ever increasing number of Methodist young people enrolled in De-Pauw University. While a sufficient amount of money has not yet been raised, a most encouraging start has been made in that direction. During the quadrennium the Methodist Orphans' Home at Lebanon has gone forward with its building program with the endorsement and backing of the Council, and now houses its children in the most comfortable way.

The State Council has given to Indiana Methodism a united voice with which to speak out in no uncertain tones upon all matters of moral reform in the state. And more than once during the quadrennium it has had occasion to speak. Recently it has been impelled to speak out in defense of that great organization for the promotion of prohibition, the Anti-Saloon League, and of its heroic leader in this state, Dr. E. S. Shumaker, who is being subjected to no end of humiliation by those who are evidently bent upon breaking down the morale of the prohibition forces in Indiana.

The Council has been exceedingly helpful in promoting the loyalty of the Area to the World Service cause. At the June session in 1924 the following challenge was given and by them accepted unanimously: "The greatest immediate problem before us is the sustaining of our benevolent work. The recent General Conference took drastic action with regard to all expenses. They cut without mercy so as to achieve every possible reduction. And they did reduce. They faced the facts and did all they could except to retreat. That, in good conscience, they could not do. And who would have wanted them to do that? We must not rob God. We must not cripple His work. But disaster is impending unless the most urgent efforts are made. Great as was our achievement five years ago, in expanding our benevolences to more worthy proportions, high as is the praise our people deserve for what has been done, can we justify retreat now? Can any personal reverses or local problems content us as a church to offer to our Lord a shrunken gift? Which orphan shall we abandon? Which patient in hospital shall we slight? Which soul shall we deny the light? Which lamb shall we starve? Which nation shall we cease to serve in keeping with the command of our Lord to carry the gospel to all the nations? No one wants to be responsible for such a tragedy, such an apostasy. But if it is to be averted, every Methodist must do his part, and do it now.

Let every subscription to the Centenary be paid as soon as possible, at the latest, by the time the Annual Conference meets. Let each pastor plead for this. Let every benevolence treasurer seek it. Let every subscriber make it a matter of holy determination. No pledge is void until paid. God will help us, we must not fail Him.

Let every member of the church subscribe to the World Service cause. Let all our pastors and laymen, without exception, organize their forces and, with the help of the Lord, address themselves to this task. Let us go forward to victory!

By the grace of God we can. Who will be responsible for anything less?"

With enthusiasm this challenge was accepted by the members of the Council and every man went back to his church with determined purpose to give a good account of his stewardship. How well the spirit of this challenge has been carried out, the benevolence record of the quadrennium will prove.

The last session of the State Council held in Indianapolis December 13, 1927, listened to the Bishop's review of the work of the quadrennium with humble thankfulness and pledged themselves to face the future with determined purpose to make the organization an even greater power for the promotion of the interests of Methodism in the Indianapolis Area.

INDIANAPOLIS AREA COUNCIL

of the

Methodist Episcopal Church

Members of the Indiana State Council

OFFICIALS

F. D. Leete, President, Resident Bishop of Indiana; C. H. Taylor, Secretary; Jesse A. Shearer, Treasurer; George M. Smith, Supt. Methodist Hospitals of Indiana; L. H. Murlin, President DePauw University; E. E. Harper, President Evansville College; E. C. Wareing, Editor, Western Christian Advocate; J. L. Stout, Supt., Children's Home; Henry Munson, Pres., Laymen's Assn., Indiana Conference; W. R. Werking, Pres., Laymen's Assn., North Indiana Conference; W. E. Carpenter, Pres., Laymen's Assn., Northwest Indiana Conference; W. B. Farmer, Secretary, Preachers Aid Society, Indiana Conference; H. L. Davis, Secretary, Preachers Aid Society, Northwest Indiana Conference; C. U. Wade, Secretary Preachers Aid Society, North Indiana Conference.

EXECUTIVE COMMITTEE

(District superintendents from all districts, one minister and one layman from each district.)

DELEGATES-AT-LARGE

Ministers—H. C. Harman, L. W. Kemper, S. L. Martin, A. E.

Monger, W. S. Bovard, E. M. Ellsworth, F. O. Fraley, E. W. Strecker, W. F. Smith.

Laymen—J. W. Esterline, J. R. Branson, M. M. Andrews, Julian Hogate, John A. Rowe, B. D. Myers, M. D., Morris Ritchie, Horace M. Kramer, E. J. W. Yerkins, Lawrence Allen, Arthur H. Sapp, Morris Clark, D. C. Turnbull.

INDIANA CONFERENCE
Bloomington District
E. H. Boldrey, C. E. Flynn, G. V. Hartman; Reserve, M. E. Abel; O. E. Anderson, E. E. Love, W. D. Ewing; Reserve, J. E. Carter.

Connersville District
J. T. Scull, Jr., L. T. Freeland, J. S. Ward, R. O. Pearson; Reserve, C. W. Whitman; C. C. Hull, Charles Birely, E. J. Hancock, Ed. H. Ruschaupt; Reserve, T. I. Sims.

Evansville District
George H. Murphy, A. E. Craig, J. M. Walker, W. T. Jones, A. J. Bigney, Roscoe Kiper, Edward McGinness, F. A. Heuring.

Indianapolis District
O. W. Fifer, J. G. Moore, E. W. Dunlavy, J. W. McFall, V. E. Rorer, George Henninger, Dwight S. Ritter, F. C. Williams, T. J. Moll, Theodore Douglas, J. V. Baker, Fred Hoke.

New Albany District
J. Edward Murr, S. J. Cross, George Dalrymple, W. E. Fisher, Robert S. Kirkham, Q. R. Hauss, R. R. Tash, Charles Brown.

Seymour District
L. C. Jeffrey, W. E. Brown, C. C. Bonnell, C. R. Stout, W. R. Stimson, C. R. Crocker, Will Green.

Vincennes District
R. H. Toole, W. H. Wylie, C. A. McCullough, W. E. Fisher; Reserve, O. E. Haley. C. R. Foutch, B. H. Yates, H. D. Hinkle; Reserve, W. E. Smith.

Mrs. Hattie L. Asbury, Corresponding Secretary W.F.M.S.; Mrs. W. S. Ennes, President, W.H.M.S.

NORTH INDIANA CONFERENCE

Ft. Wayne District

W. W. Wiant, G. F. Hubbartt, O. T. Martin, Edward Antle. A. B. Cline, Loring Scott, Dr. M. F. Steele, D. F. Shannon.

Goshen District

C. H. Smith, C. G. Yeomans, J. S. Newcombe, C. A. McPheeters; Reserve, R. J. Hutsinpiller. Frank Greene, S. L. Poor, D. C. Turnbull; Reserve, S. F. DePoy.

Logansport District

L. C. Bentley, A. H. Backus, C. W. Montgomery, A. K. Love; Reserve, R. L. Wilson. Charles W. Beecher, Tracy Hollingsworth, Fred Beauchamp, Lloyd McClure; Reserve, D. M. McCoy.

Muncie District

W. T. Arnold, C. M. Fawns, L. G. Jacobs, W. E. Hamilton; Reserve, J. W. Rose. W. H. Forse, W. E. Waggoner, William Lewis, A. E. Bauer; Reserve, O. L. Menon.

Richmond District

F. F. Thornburg, J. Ira Jones, L. W. Kemper; Reserve, U. S. Hartley. George T. Whitaker, M. H. Gaar, Russell McHatten; Reserve, W. G. Batt.

Wabash District

U. S. A. Bridge, F. K. Dougherty, J. F. Edwards; Reserve, Herbert Boase. M. B. Stults, M. D. Foland, G. C. Diztler; Reserve, O. J. Neighbours.

Mrs. W. R. Werking, Corresponding Secretary W. F. M. S.; Mrs. F. F. Thornburg, President, W. H. M. S.

NORTHWEST INDIANA CONFERENCE

Crawfordsville District

O. T. Martin, F. L. Hovis, H. P. Ivey, Guy O. Carpenter, Frank Evans, Henry Shobe, Ben F. McKey; Howard Cann.

Greencastle District

A. T. Briggs, Benj. Rist, C. H. Taylor, J. E. Porter, Henry W. Bopp, W. M. Blanchard, W. E. Ferguson, W. E. Carpenter.

Lafayette District

J. J. Wilson, T. F. Williams, R. H. Crowder, M. C. Hunt, O. B. Smith, J. J. Hunt, R. H. Shook, O. M. Tuggle; Reserve, Harvey Smith.

South Bend District

B. D. Beck, W. G. Seaman, A. H. Kenna, V. B. Servies, C. O. Holmes, J. M. Chillas, J. A. Secor, Samuel Schlosser.

Mrs. Mary Ostrom, President, W.H.M.S.; Mrs. Ida H. Clyne, Corresponding Secretary, W.F.M.S.

SOUTHERN ILLINOIS CONFERENCE

Officials

Cameron Harmon, President, McKendree College; C. C. Hall, Superintendent Orphanage.

Carbondale District

W. M. Brown, A. R. Ransom, Robert Morris, B. H. Batson, M. S. Carter, C. H. Mitchell, J. P. Roe.

Centralia District

C. B. Whiteside, M. H. Loar, J. D. Shaddrick, J. J. Brown, C. F. Pruett, S. B. Vaughn.

East St. Louis District

W. H. Whitlock, L. S. McKown, Frank F. Otto, C. R. Yost; Reserve, M. A. Souers. Leonard Carson, Al Harper, Mildred Trabue.

Mt. Carmel District

C. L. Peterson, O. B. Allen, Geo. R. Goodman; Reserve, C. D. Shumard. J. M. Mitchell, Will Johnson, Homer Young.

Olney District

F. O. Wilson, Ressho Robertson, W. E. Bennett, N. E. Prince, J. S. Abbott.

WOMEN'S WORK.

By Mrs. Madison Swadener.

Since the year 1807, when the first authentic facts of the origin of Methodism in Indiana came to light, the hand of Methodist womanhood has ably cooperated to mold the raw material of the saddle-bag days into the great and advancing institution of the Methodist Episcopal Church of Indiana, whose ever-extending activities and progress are recorded in this second quadrennial report.

In the pioneer days Methodist women labored in a stern environment and under rugged hardships. The homely log cabin was a place of sacrifice, its hearth the Altar of God, and its four walls the seat of learning. From this lonely home Methodism was reared and the influence of that home has played its part in the onward march of our present day church.

Today, the women of Methodism are playing the same vital part. Conditions have changed, and the scope of their activities and the horizon of their service has extended from cabin to state and nation, and finally to world-wide consecration and leadership.

The organization of the Woman's Foreign Missionary Society claims our attention from the time of its inception in 1869, when Isabella Thoburn was sent to India with its valiant work for the Church of Jesus Christ. The women of Indiana Methodism have reared their children in the fear of God and planted in their hearts a desire to live unselfish lives. When the call for organization came they quickly responded both for local service and for the spreading of the Gospel in foreign fields.

Many who were pioneers in the work have gone to their reward. For twenty years Mrs. Hattie L. Asbury has been the efficient, consecrated secretary in the Indiana Conference. To work for her Master is her meat and drink. Mrs. Anna B. Adams has a longer record of service, giving thirty-three years as treasurer. These women are loved for their leadership and long service.

Enthusiasm and growth are shown for the quadrennium. The figures given tell only in part of what has been accomplished, for back of them is the great heart of woman and her love for humanity. Missionaries, Bible Women, scholarships, and special work are made possible by the women who are responsible for the work of the Woman's Foreign Missionary Society of the Indianapolis Area. The membership of this society totals 52,668, including children.

The receipts of the conferences of the Indianapolis Area for the past quadrennium were as follows:

Indiana Conference		Northwest Indiana	
1924	$61,158.00	1924	$38,065.00
1925	66,132.00	1925	35,370.00
1926	66,499.00	1926	32,643.00
1927	70,681.00	1927	35,750.00
	$263,470.00		$141,848.00

North Indiana		Southern Illinois	
1924	$46,286.00	1924	$24,188.00
1925	46,909.00	1925	$25,196.00
1926	47,250.00	1926	26,216.00
1927	48,274.00	1927	21,930.00
	$188,719.00		$97,521.00

The call to organize for work in the homeland met with the same response from women whose lives were given to God's service who heard the call,

"From street and square, from hill and glen,
The tread of marching men
The patient armies of the poor."

The women of Indiana mobilized to meet the call and have pressed on through discouragements with unfaltering steps. Today these two great connectional societies of Methodism stand shoulder to shoulder in this Area, and by their strong faith have clasped hands with other workers around the globe, belting it with Gospel Light.

The activities of the Woman's Home Missionary Society in Indiana are outstanding in a section of Fort Wayne, where the new and splendidly equipped settlement building, known as the Kate

Bilderback Neighborhood House, is rendering real Christian and social service among more than seven thousand foreign workers. The Campbell settlement in Gary, Indiana, is helping to solve the needs for the foreign population in that rapidly growing industrial center. East St. Louis, with its complete settlement house deserves notice for the work they are accomplishing among the children of that section.

In considering the work of the Woman's Home Missionary Society, the active work of Methodist women in support of the Methodist hospitals of Indiana is outstanding. In this connection Mrs. Frederick D. Leete, wife of the Bishop of the Area, as president of the Hospital Guild, has been untiring in her efforts in behalf of these institutions.

Mention should be made of our deaconesses, working under the Woman's Home Missionary Society, who are giving their lives in constant service for the sick and unfortunate, doing city mission work, working among the miners, teaching Bible classes, and serving as pastors' assistants. These worthy servants are working out from the Indianapolis Deaconess Home which at present is inadequate, and the purchase of a new home is planned. The total membership of this society is 48,978, including children.

The financial report for the past quadrennium follows:

Indiana Conference		North Indiana Conference	
1924	$29,726.36	1924	$35,213.02
1925	23,658.11	1925	34,873.75
1926	30,417.16	1926	34,159.99
1927	31,689.37	1927	37,023.77
	$115,491.00		$141,270.53

Northwest Indiana Conference		Southern Illinois Conference	
1924	$15,098.87	1924	$14,349.93
1925	15,161.38	1925	14,599.97
1926	15,686.10	1926	15,101.10
1927	16,889.38	1927	15,865.77
	$62,835.73		$59,914.77

INSTITUTE, CAMPUS
McKENDREE COLLEGE
LEBANON
ILLINOIS

AUDITORIUM
EPWORTH
FOREST
INDIANA

EPWORTH FOREST
HOTEL
INDIANA

BATTLE GROUND
ASSEMBLY HOTEL
INDIANA

RIVERVALE, INDIANA
AUDITORIUM

GLIMPSES OF EPWORTH INSTITUTES

During this quadrennium the joint societies of the missionary branches have established a second school of missions at Rivervale, Indiana. This in connection with the mission school established at Battle Ground during the past quadrennium is accomplishing much for missions.

This brief history of Methodist women must consider the Ladies' Aid Society. From the inception of Methodism the women of this society have labored hand in hand with pastors and laymen in raising thousands of dollars in the construction, furnishing, and repairing of church equipment. Their efforts are directly connected with the growth of Methodism in Indiana and cannot be separated from its militant advance.

Methodist women have also pioneered in the cause of temperance. Since the formation of the Woman's Christian Temperance Union in November, 1897 they have ever been in the front rank of the fight and their vigilance has never been challenged.

We have pictured in a limited way some of the achievements of Methodist women. They are now serving as pastors, teachers in Sunday schools, members of quarterly conferences, instructors and professors in our colleges, and as members of the General Conference. Their purpose is to bear some part in the evangelization of the world, to bring about that glad, good time when "The wilderness, and the solitary place shall be glad; and the desert shall rejoice and blossom as the rose."

Many of our women have ended their labors -- some long ago, others in more recent years, "and their works do follow them." They were women of Methodism. We, too, are women of Methodism, like them toiling to advance the Master's Kingdom, and working in our own spheres of privilege and duty to help bring the world to Christ.

CITY COUNCILS

By Rev. R. R. Detweiler

In the "World Tomorrow," for October, 1927, is an amazing article on "The Trend Toward Consolidation." Institutions and industries are joining hands.

The Methodist Church in many cities of our state has not been slow to see the importance of such management. This movement has been given special impetus during the present Area administration.

The Councils in the Indianapolis Area differ in name and somewhat in plans and purposes, but the underlying motive and effort is very much the same. There is the felt need of certain Christian enterprises that have no visible financial support. There is a growing sense of the strength of unified effort. Certain things can be accomplished that otherwise would be impossible. A fine fellowship is promoted between Methodist groups.

The Indianapolis Council was organized in 1923. This new organization at once took over the Methodist Union and proceeded with definitely outlined plans. Six objects were stated:

First—To make surveys of new and rapidly growing sections of the city.

Second—Decide upon and secure well located sites in new communities.

Third—Receive donations of money and property for city missionary use.

Fourth—Assume custody of weak or abandoned churches, that all assets may be conserved.

Fifth—Establish Sunday schools and church activities, and help to maintain them until they are able to assume self-support.

Sixth—Secure public presentation of the needs, opportunities, plans and programs of the Council in all the Methodist congregations in the city.

The membership is composed of laymen and ministers from the various churches, based on the comparative membership in each.

The society has grown slowly but steadily. A project for building a central community building adjoining Fletcher Place and combining the Methodist Settlement work there has been inaugurated. Churches of the city have been helped in building enterprises, and in a couple of instances the lots were originally purchased by the Council.

The South Bend City Missionary Society considers questions of city-wide and local church interest. Here there is rather a dual organization, but the two function as one in their building program. There is a joint quarterly conference, second and third quarters, of the Methodist churches.

The society is helping the Sacred Heart Mission (Hungarian) in its fine program in the city. Building enterprises are presented to the various congregations where finances are difficult or impossible. The city has been divided among the churches in missionary responsibility asking certain churches to develop the section assigned.

Every Methodist church in the city comprises the Missionary society and of course participates in the joint quarterly conference. Some outstanding speaker is usually procured for these conferences and some phase of the work presented.

In Kokomo, the Council is called the "Social Union." The Union has sponsored the building of two churches costing $25,-000—Trinity and Parr Memorial. Their combined membership is over 200, with a Sunday school enrollment of 376 and an average of 253. The Union pledged $12,000 and has already paid $8,000.

At Terre Haute it is called the "Federated Council." The organization is composed of two members from each local Methodist church. Four or five meetings have been held to which the members of the official boards and their families have been invited. They have been very successful.

Perhaps the most outstanding thing accomplished has been in relocating one of the churches and assisting it to attain position in a new and well-equipped building.

In Fort Wayne the Council has been christened "The Methodist Union of the Methodist Episcopal Church." Its purpose, as outlined in the constitution, is the organization and aid of church and Sunday schools; the erection of buildings; the conducting of missions and schools; the support of institutions for the relief of the destitute; the recovery of the outcasts; and the unifying of the churches in the operation of the spiritual life.

The union has been incorporated in order that it may hold property. The membership includes pastors and members of the several Quarterly Conferences and Superintendents of Missions and Institutions, and not to exceed two members from each.

Offerings are taken annually by each of the churches of the city and an effort is made to coordinate all Methodism's activities. It is organized as auxiliary to the Department of City Work of the Board of Home Missions and Church Extension of the Methodist Episcopal Church.

Several other of the larger communities of the state have taken steps or are making plans for doing coordinated work along the lines outlined above. Plans are under way for a Calumet Methodist Union. There was at one time such a union but it has not been in operation for some time and there is a need now.

Lafayette has no council at present, but some of the machinery for such an organization has been started.

Evansville does not have a council, but once a month the ministers of the Evansville district meet in the city and take up such matters as are of especial interest to all.

In reviewing the work of the Methodist church throughout the state, it is evident that there is an increasing emphasis upon "consolidated" effort. In the larger cities, the impact of the Methodism is distinctly felt through these movements and that impact is always for a better individual and community life.

The Wayne Street, Fort Wayne, Church House was formally dedicated by Bishop Frederick D. Leete, on May 20th, 1923. The building furnishes excellent equipment for the work of the church school and will furnish splendid facilities for taking care of the various committees, the book room, and numerous activities of the annual conference session.

THE CARE OF OUR VETERAN PREACHERS

By W. B. Farmer, D.D., Secretary, Preachers' Aid Society,
Indiana Conference.

Southern Illinois Conference.

The amount of funds on hand at the beginning of the quadrennium was $135,689.00. There has been added during the quadrennium $33,276.00. There has been no special drive but a constant and careful looking after prospects by the officers and friends of the Conference Claimants Society. The president, Mr. J. M. Mitchell of Mount Carmel, Illinois, says, "It has been the easiest fund to accumulate in which we have had any part." The conference is paying its claimants $22.00 for each year of service. The matter of gathering new funds is chiefly in charge of the laymen of the conference.

In addition to these funds there is a Preachers' Mutual Benefit Association in the conference, which is a burial mutual through which a stipulated amount is paid to each widow upon the death of her husband.

North Indiana Conference.

Rev. C. U. Wade, the General Secretary of the Preachers' Aid Society of the North Indiana Conference reports that at the beginning of the quadrennium the society had $635,400.00 in resources. The results of the special campaign for raising funds and subscriptions during the quadrennium were $157,000.00. The present assets of the society at the close of the quadrennium are $794,495.00. The rate of annuity paid to claimants in 1923 was $21.00; in 1927 it was $25.00. The conference has voted in favor of the ideal of the pension reserve plan, with the expectation that it will be adjusted in some details by the General Conference. The society pays annual annuities on $170,000.00 of annuity bonds.

Indiana Conference.

The former quadrennium closed with a report of $378,448.00 in assets in the two treasuries of the Preachers' Aid Society and the Veteran's Home Society of the Indiana conference. The report in 1927 shows resources of $723,068.00 in the two societies. The increase in income from these funds has grown during the quadrennium from $10,326.00 to $15,520.00, and the annuity rate paid increased from $17.00 per year of service to $20.00. The present total resources of the society including wills, estate notes and pledges amount to a little more than $805,000.00. During the quadrennium $123,398.00 cash has been collected. The society is paying annuity on $56,000.00. Rev. W. B. Farmer, secretary of the society, has had charge of the campaign. The expectation is to build the endowment funds to at least $1,000,000. The Indiana Conference has approved of the principle of the proposed Pension Reserve Plan and looks with favor upon its adoption.

Northwest Indiana Conference.

This is one of the few conferences of Methodism that pay the full legal claim of the retired minister, and has been doing so for the last two quadrenniums. The rate of annuity paid in 1923 was $25.00, and in 1927 was $27.00. The funds for this are gathered from the interest on endowment and collections from the churches and pastors, together with the usual checks from other general church funds. At the beginning of the quadrennium the permanent funds were $225,681.00. During the quadrennium the principle and plan of the pension reserve system was unanimously endorsed by the conference, and Dr. Henry L. Davis, one of the experienced leaders of the conference, was made the secretary of the Preachers' Aid Society and sent out to raise funds with which to commute the obligations of the conference into the new fund. In three years $200,000.00 has been added to the fund which, when the conference shall adopt the plan, will be used to commute this claim.

Thus it will be seen that throughout the Area during this quadrennium there has been a decided growth in the interest and concern for the veteran preacher and his widow and orphan, and each conference is making practical and well planned steps to take better care of this faithful servant of the church in the future. The writer believes it fair to say that in all of these conferences the matter has become a living concern of the church and that there will be a very decided improvement in this condition during the next quadrennium because of the careful preparations made and the movements put under way during these four years.

A NEW DEPARTURE IN CHURCH ARCHITECTURE.

By Joseph B. Rosemurgy, B.D.

In recent years there has been manifested in the Methodist Episcopal Church and other so-called non-liturgical churches, tendencies toward the creation in brick and stone of buildings that inspire worship. In the past many of our Methodist churches have not supplied all that art and architecture, in beauty of design and arrangement and color might offer as a fitting symbolism of the presence of a God of truth, holiness, perfection and love. Upon entering many of the churches erected in years past it is much easier to think of them as assembly rooms rather than sanctuaries, meeting houses rather than temples of the soul, with their bare walls and austere environment for the preaching of the Word and the fellowship of believers. In justice, however, to our Methodist past which has registered so much of great glorious achievement, it should be said that from these centers of unattractive church architecture there have gone forth through the years multitudes of men and women who, baptized by the power of the Spirit, were committed to the great task and ideal of enthroning Christ in the life of the world. All honor to those of yesterday who in the small and unadorned meeting house saw the vision splendid and translated its meaning into terms of sacrificial endeavors.

The change which in many places has come over the form and decoration of our church buildings will be welcomed by all who recognize what a large contribution suggestive architecture, with its beauty of design, can make to the atmosphere of worship. Approaching a typical modern church edifice, several of which have been erected in the Indianapolis Area during the past eight years, one is impressed with the idea of beauty, durability, strength and spaciousness. There is in clear outline in most of these, a reflection of the Gothic type of architecture which so perfectly identifies itself with the real meaning of worship.

That beautiful symbolism so evident in the Gothic type of the Old World is beginning to impress itself upon the religious life of the New World. New temples, like poems in brick and stone, erected for the glory of God and dedicated to Him for the high purpose of worship, occupy commanding positions in city, town and village. Upon entering these Methodist sanctuaries one is greeted with an interior that in arrangement and furnishings suggest the ideal worship environment. There are auditoriums with architectural features that suggest the garish, the artificial and the theatrical. At times our auditoriums have unfortunately been reduced to the psychology of the forum and theatre. A new and greater day has dawned for the worship life of the church when the sanctuary in all its appointments leads the worshiper to feel as the psalmist felt for the House of God.

In such churches as these, pictures of some of which appear in this book, the chancel is the central and crowning feature. A new departure has come in the design of the chancel of our churches. In its arrangement it is simplified, and altogether conducive to the spirit of reverence and worship. In the chancel there are four great symbols of the religious life, each having its logical position in the sanctuary. First, there is the baptismal font, representing the initial step in Christian discipleship, a fitting symbol of the portal to the fellowship of kindred souls. Second, there stands the reading desk or lectern, for the presentation of the written Word of God with its ministry to inquiring minds and eager hearts. Third, there is the pulpit, the place of the prophet of the Lord, where the great and glorious truths of the gospel of the grace of God are proclaimed for the salvation of men and the edifying of believers. Fourth, and perhaps the most important of all is the communion table, a symbol in itself of the great sacrifice which expresses the idea and ideal of Christian fellowship. The only proper place for the table of the Lord is the central focal point, subordinating it to nothing in its position.

It can be said of this new departure in the interior arrangement of the sanctuary that where it obtains it restores the altar to its rightful place in the worship life of the Church. When the worshiper enters the House of God, his eyes should see, not first the organ with its prominent pipes occupying a commanding position or the preacher occupying the center of the platform, but the impressive symbol of Calvary with all its suggestive meaning for the life of the world. The presence of these four symbols of the Christian faith in the modern simplified chancel creates an atmosphere of worship and makes the church a potential House of Prayer.

NEW CHURCH BUILDINGS.

This has been a quadrennium of church building, even as was the quadrennium preceding it. It may be said that during the eight year period now closing the physical equipment of Methodism within the Indianapolis Area has been practically transformed. This section had fallen somewhat behind in the size, quality, and utility of its church buildings. That condition is now rapidly being righted and the Indianapolis Area is well on its way toward a foremost place in the matter of material equipment.

The new churches in the Area are all mentioned specifically in the various district reports in this volume. An examination of these statements alone will indicate how great has been the activity in the construction of new churches and parsonages and how courageous the Methodist people of the Area have been in assuming financial responsibilities for houses of worship and accommodations for pastors and their families. The total expended runs into a large figure and the economy in the construction of churches is such that probably the actual value of these properties represents a still larger figure. Especially notable in the list of new churches completed during the quadrennium are: Broadway and Irvington Churches, Indianapolis; City Church, Gary; First Church, Greensburg; Waynedale Church, Fort Wayne; Madison Avenue Church, Muncie; and the new churches at Beech Grove; Hartford City; Chesterton; and Erie, Indiana, the last two being rural churches.

A glance at the few of these new church buildings pictured in this volume will indicate an improvement in architectural taste and standards for church building which would also be borne out by an examination of all the buildings recently completed. The churches being built today are at once more beautiful, more in accordance with accepted architectural types, and more adequate for a practical community service. It is highly worth while that our people are making progress in the artistic sense and in the larger conception of the social opportunity of the church. Europe has churches that have been the admiration of discerning eyes for centuries. America is also beginning to build up such a combined heritage of religious and artistic values. In the years to come the Indianapolis Area will contribute its share.

One of the early dreams of the leaders of Israel was that of a suitable house to shelter the occasion of worship. One king was moved to such a plan by what seemed to him the injustice of the fact that he lived in a palace while the dwelling place of Jehovah was but a tent. The Indianapolis Area gives evidence of an awakened desire that that part of human life which definitely relates to the personality of God shall be adequately and pleasingly housed. This will greatly hasten the progress of the Kingdom itself, for the cultured mind and the sensitive spirit delight a little more in the service of God when it is carried on in an attractive place.

NEW COMMUNITY BUILDINGS.

The fact that the Christian consciousness and the church's conception of service have grown is evidenced by the constant increase in the number and value of community buildings in connection with churches. This present day manifestation of the church's interest in humanity has had a large place in the development of the Indianapolis Area during the quadrennium now closing. In many of the city churches, in some of the churches in small towns, and in at least a few of the strictly rural churches this adaptation to community needs and interests has been brought to a material realization.

The new community buildings built during the quadrennium will be found especially mentioned in the section of this book contributed by the district superintendents. Their cost will also be found stated there and it will be noted that the amount expended on them is a considerable one. Especially notable in the list are the community buildings in connection with First Church, Goshen; Trinity Church, Evansville; Wall Street Church, Jeffersonville; and Wayne Street Church, Fort Wayne, Indiana.

While it might be said that the community unit development in Methodism is still in the experimental stage, it is also to be said that thus far the experiment has been successful. This is indicated by the fact that an increasing number of churches are erecting or planning such units for their equipment.

All of this grows out of the increasingly well realized fact that the church is something more than an institution. It is a religious community. It is not a group withdrawing itself from the life of the world, but one attempting the rebuilding of the life of the world on a plan harmonizing with the spirit of the Christian religion. It is the people worshiping together, serving together, eating together, laughing together, and uniting in Christian friendship and sociability. It is Christianity reaching out to touch the life of the world at all of its normal points and in all its essential interests.

In other words the attempt of the church today is to minister not to a department of life, but to life in its totality. Details may yet have to be adjusted and minor problems solved but it seems certain that the principle involved is correct and permanent.

THE WESTERN CHRISTIAN ADVOCATE

By Ernest C. Wareing, D.D., L.H.D., Editor.

The Western Christian Advocate is the official organ of the Indianapolis and Cincinnati Areas. It is now in its ninety-fourth year of service. Established in 1834 it has witnessed and borne testimony to the growth of state and nation through the most remarkable period in the world's history. During the past quadrennium it has maintained an enviable record in its circulation. At the present time it stands second among the Advocates, following the New York, and far in advance of those following it. This position has been consistently held during the four years, terminating with the coming General Conference. The total subscribers from the Indianapolis Area according to Conferences is:

Indiana Conference 6,185
North Indiana 5,519
Northwest Indiana 2,152
Southern Illinois 1,428

Aggregate subscriptions of Indianapolis Area......15,284

The subscription list of the North Indiana Conference is worthy of special mention. It leads all others of the two Areas and carries the largest per capita circulation to the church paper of any conference in Methodism.

The service rendered by the paper has been of extensive value. It has supported the policy and program of the Bishops and of the District Superintendents and of the pastors to the limit of space and ability. It has furnished publicity for all the benevolent institutions, and has carried the connectional life of the Church in every issue, holding this as the dominant motive for promoting the interests of the Kingdom of God.

Two important results of the work for the quadrennium should be mentioned.

First, the paper during each year of this period has been without a deficit. It has made money.

Second, the paper has become the organ for the Southland covering the field of the Southeastern Christian Advocate, which became an edition of the Western to be issued during the last two and one-half months of this quadrennium as the "Southern Edition of the Western Christian Advocate."

EPWORTH LEAGUE INSTITUTES

B. T. F. Williams, D.D.

The Epworth league Institute is one of the modern features of Methodism. There are four such organizations in the area, and each is doing a work of increasing value to the church.

The McKendree Institute located at Lebanon, Illinois, is held on the beautiful campus of McKendree College. A place more appropriate or more conducive to learning and inspiration could not be found. The ground has become historic and sacred to Methodists because of the work of Cartwright and McKendree who wrought valiantly there.

Rivervale in the Indiana Conference is one of the most intriguing places in the state for a gathering of young people. A short while ago there were no structures of any kind on the grounds, but the enterprise of Methodist leadership is here expressed. The landscape artist pointed out the possibilities, and now there are sweeping drives, cottages, dormitories, a steel tabernacle, and attractive camping sites.

Epworth Forest on the northern shore of Lake Webster has the distinction of being the largest institute of Methodism. Four years ago there were no buildings. Four hundred and twenty-eight lots have now been sold, and beautiful summer cottages are on hillside and lake shore. A splendid summer hotel has been constructed, and an auditorium with a seating capacity of twenty-five hundred adorns a hill crest. There is ample room for athletic fields, and a landscape of unusual beauty. Epworth Forest lends itself to a joyous educational and inspirational atmosphere.

Battle Ground is the oldest institute of the area. Organized fifteen years ago it has enjoyed achievement from the beginning. The grounds are adjacent to the Tippecanoe battlefield which is seven miles from Lafayette. The camp has more than fifty cottages, district dormitories, a modern hotel, a spacious tabernacle, space for tents, athletic fields and a swimming pool. Through the generous gift of seventy acres of land by Mr. and Mrs. J. W. Harrison of Attica, Indiana, to the Battle Ground Assembly, an artificial lake is a part of the present program. The camp is shaded by great oaks and modest maples.

These summer gatherings employ on an average ninety-four instructors. They are selected men and women from all quarters of the church. Ministers, college professors and missionaries for the most part make up the faculties. The work is presented with such dedication to a great task that at the close of the week youth never fails to see the duties and opportunities of life in wider measure than before.

The course of study is much the same in all institutes. The morning watch, Bible study, missions, methods, vocational guidance, personal problems, Methodism, evangelism, citizenship, hymnology and the forum as a usual thing have an hour in every schedule. The afternoon is largely given over to recreation and games. The evening hour is one suitable to a busy day of study and play.

One feature of the institute is the Camp Fire service on Saturday evening. Here much of the work of the week becomes manifest. There are testimonies, requests for prayer and oftentimes decisions for some form of life service. On Sunday morning usually about ten o'clock comes the registration service at which youth publicly makes known its religious purpose. This is not an occasion of great excitement, but one in which young people are asked to face the implications of religious decision, and to accept them with cool calculation. Aside from definite life choices, oftentimes unconverted young people take the first step in the Christian life.

The actual results of the institute during the quadrennium are difficult to summarize. The registration for that period has been 15,550, and more than 3,000 young people have made some form of religious decision during the four years work. The intangible values are more than figures could show. There have been the finest social contacts under healthful surroundings, and there have been intellectual and spiritual stimulations which can never be weighed. Out from these institutes have gone scores of young people who are becoming leaders in their local churches, and who will "carry on" tomorrow. "The Epworth League Institute is the Camp Meeting modernized."

INDIANAPOLIS AREA METHODISM AND REFORM

By E. Robb Zaring, D.D.

The Methodist Episcopal Church, closely associated as she has been from the beginning with the mass of the American people, has naturally been interested in the broader phases of religion as they affect the social, political and economic aspects of community and national life. This fact offers a suggestion as to why the social creed of American Protestantism was first conceived by a body of Methodist ministers, adopted by our own church as its social creed, and later taken over by the Federal Council of Churches. From the very beginning her ministers and laymen have been prominent in all movements calculated to produce a better soil and a cleaner atmosphere in which to grow and develop individual and social righteousness.

The heart of the church is largely reflected in the character and attitude of its public servants on social and reform subjects. A survey of Methodist men of affairs within the bounds of the Indianapolis Area during the past few years affords but an exemplification of our opening statements. Governor J. Frank Hanly was not only active in temperance reform, but his was the only administration that dared to lift a protesting voice against the presence of organized and thoroughly intrenched gambling at French Lick; it was an unsuccessful protest but it revealed the spirit of the man.

The late Senator Beveridge was a prominent advocate of the present Primary Law. He was also foremost in the matter of child labor reform, being the author of a national child labor bill that became a law, but was declared unconstitutional by supreme court decision.

Wherever a vigorous and progressive Methodist church is found, there will be discovered a reform agency, a savor of righteousness; and there will probably also be found a Methodist preacher in the forefront of local reform movements.

It is in the field of temperance reform that Indianapolis Area Methodism has labored most persistently and successfully, from the days of Dr. Thomas A. Goodwin, whose pungent pen was active and whose voice was never stilled, down to the late Col. Eli F. Ritter, who virtually abandoned a lucrative law practice to give himself without stint to reform. He was responsible for the law that a saloon in a residential district is a menace per se. He also drafted the famous Nicholson Law, and was a factor in the convention that launched the movement that resulted in the Eighteenth Amendment. The late Hon. Thomas Moore of Greencastle was the author of the Moore Remonstrance Law, making it possible to close saloons by petition. Mr. R. C. Minton, for fifteen years counsel for the Indiana Anti-Saloon League, drafted the bone-dry, county option, statewide prohibition, and other dry measures passed by the state legislature up to the year 1925.

In the state work of the League the following field workers are Methodists: The Rev. Messrs. H. W. Baldridge, W. M. Whitsitt, Leroy Huddleston, Frank W. Loy and E. S. Shumaker, also the Hon. L. E. York, and Clark F. Rogers. At the 1928 State Convention of the League when nearly two thousand delegates registered, the strength of Methodism was quite evident; of the forty-five Field Day services held in connection with the meeting twenty-seven were held in Methodist churches. We mention these facts with no other purpose or spirit than to indicate the uncompromising attitude of the church on this, the greatest of all reforms.

Any reference to reform work within the Indianapolis Area without naming E. S. Shumaker, D.D., who for the past quarter of a century has been a leader in the prohibition movement, would be wholly incomplete. Dr. Shumaker has served as State Superintendent of the Indiana Anti-Saloon League for the past twenty-one years. He has been so aggressive and successful in the prosecution of the reform as to feel the force of a ruthless opposition that has sought to end his usefulness. These attacks have only served to bring forth the practically unanimous and unqualified support of the Protestant population and upstanding organizations of the state.

All the ministers and laymen mentioned in these paragraphs are members of the Methodist Episcopal Church and but typify the spirit of the church. Methodism has a message of salvation for the individual, as is indicated by the high place held by the Area in the increase of members and the number of conversions. She also seeks to heal the soul and body of society. Methodism is salt, and it would be a day to be deplored should she lose her savor. There is a Christ of the Indiana Road, a road that must be transformed into a highway whereon her people may travel without fear of the ravenous beast of organized evil.

INDIANAPOLIS AREA METHODISM IN THE GENERAL CHURCH

By Freeland A. Hall, D.D.

Indianapolis Area Methodism, born in pioneer days under the inspirational leadership of men like Peter Cartwright, George Horn, Jesse Haile, and Nathan Robertson, fostered a movement that was continued by Richard Hargrave, James Havens, and Allen Wiley, and has contributed its full share to world redemption. These flaming evangels, unacquainted with wires and wire-

EVANSVILLE COLLEGE

HISTORIC CHAPEL
McKENDREE COLLEGE

NEW TAYLOR UNIVERSITY
DORMITORIES

LONGDEN HALL
DEPAUW UNIVERSITY

CAMPUS VIEWS

less, preached the gospel message to the sturdy pioneers, and each sympathetic hearer became a vibrant loud speaker, giving the message to the world parish.

Among the Area educators who have contributed to the general good must be mentioned Cyrus Nutt, first preceptor at Indiana Asbury University, and later president of Indiana University. To this list of builders should be added the names of Thomas Bowman, Matthew Simpson, Edwin H. Hughes, Francis J. McConnell, and George R. Grose, the last last three now bishops of the church. Other men who were born, educated, or have served the church here and have been elected to the office of bishop are: Robert R. Roberts, first bishop resident in Indiana; Isaac W. Joyce; Earl Cranston, member of Indiana Conference in 1874-1875; Edward R. Ames, sometime publishing agent of the church; William O. Shepard, and Fred B. Fisher, for a time missionary to India. Evelyn Riley Nicholson, wife of Bishop Nicholson, is one of Indiana's daughters.

Other Methodist educators whose influence has extended to a large field are: W. S. Bovard, secretary of the Board of Education; William H. Hickman, William G. Seaman, Alfred E. Craig. Joseph W. VanCleve, Alfred H. Hughes, John F. Harmon, Hilary A. Gobin, Harry A. King, Edwin W. Dunlavy, Henry B. Longden, Andrew Bigney, William W. Sweet, Fred W. Hixson, William M. Blanchard, John P. D. John, H. B. Gough, Lemuel H. Murlin, Charles W. Lewis, William E. Smyser, John H. T. Main, Louis G. Adkinson, Marion Rex Trabue, William L. Sanders, L. N. Hines, L. A. Pittenger, Roy P. Wisehart, David Shaw Duncan and Edwin Post.

Among the editors, authors and writers of Indiana Methodism we find: Edward and George Carey Eggleston, Freeman D., George F., and Charles L. Bovard, Albion Fellows Bacon, Annie Fellows Johnston, Harvey Reeves Calkins, George B. Lockwood, John Clark Ridpath, Albert J. Beveridge and William H. Mace, historians; Ernest C. Wareing, editor of the Western Christian Advocate from 1916. Worth M. Tippy, Frank G. Browne, Jeremiah H. Bayliss, and E. Robb Zaring, assistant editor Western and editor for twelve years of the Northwestern Christian Advocate.

Other Methodists who have exercised an influence in Christian service in ecclesiastical affairs are: R. J. Wade, secretary of World

Service commission; Blaine E. Kirkpatrick, general secretary of the Epworth League; and Wilbur F. Sheridan, one time general secretary of the Epworth League.

Nearly three hundred missionaries have gone into foreign service from the Indianapolis Area. Among these torch-bearers of an early day were: J. Howell Pyke, W. F. Walker, Thomas Bond Wood, John Ing, and Ella C. Shaw. More recent missionary representatives are: W. W. Lockwood (Y.M.C.A. China), Preston S. Hyde, Carl H. Conley, Joshua F. Cottingham, J. O. Swain, William A. Shelley, Marie Adams, Bernice Bassett, "Ted" Mumby and Dr. Rebecca Parrish.

Authors and teachers of general influence in the realm of science who should be named are Melvin I. Cook, Charles W. Hargitt, Arthur L. Foley, Robert E. Lyons, William F. Book, Paul Weatherwax and Burton D. Myers.

Other Indianapolis Area men who have made large contributions to the general good are: Colonel Eli F. Ritter, attorney; Arthur H. Sapp, International President of Rotary. Washington C. DePauw, Hugh Dougherty, Edward Rector, Clement Studebaker, B. F. and W. H. Adams, Marvin Campbell and Albert B. Cline are notable as philanthropists.

METHODISM IN PUBLIC LIFE

By Chas. H. Neff

To write the story of the Methodists of this Area who have served the state or the nation is almost to write the history of Indiana. Even before there were any regularly organized churches, Methodists were serving in the pioneer communities and from that distant day even to the present time, the members of our great church have taken their place in the councils of the state and nation.

It would be an almost endless task and one which would require volumes to tell of all of the members of the church who have thus served. The first community governments, the first constitutional convention, the first legislature, the first state officials, all of these had Methodists among their number and some of them attained more than ordinary notice. This may be in part because of the number of Methodists. Certainly it may also be said that it is because Methodism breeds men in whom the citizenry may place their confidence.

Those men who helped shape the destiny of Indiana by their activity deserve great honor. Among them, we may name Dennis Pennington and Hugh Cull, John DePauw, James P. Burgess, Isaac Dunn, T. A. Goodwin, John C. Moore, Davis Floyd, James Conwell, Hosier J. Durbin, Calvin W. Ruter, Samuel Brenton, Calvin Fletcher, William Hendricks, third governor of Indiana, and Amos Lane. Some of these men were ministers and all of them took some important part in forming the new state's government and welfare. And this list does not name that great number who served in some smaller but equally important position. It cannot tell of the legion who served their own communities with equal fidelity and equal honor.

The second constitutional convention and the succeeding period which brought with it the Great Conflict also shows its share of Methodist men bearing the burdens of state and pointing the course of the body politic. Not merely were there then civil officers but the great army which went forth to defend the Union was filled with members of our church who did not forget their allegiance to God and His church.

This list is long, and shining out in golden letters may be seen the names of Gen. T. A. Morris, Gilbert De La Matyr, W. C. De-Pauw, Prof. M. J. Fletcher, James Whitcomb, twice governor of Indiana and United States Senator; Joseph A. Wright, twice governor, United States Senator and minister to Berlin; Elisha Embree, Robert W. Thompson, jurist and congressman; W. C. Larrabee and G. W. Hoss, state superintendents of education; John C. Moore, John M. Alcott, Samuel R. Adams, Dr. William B. Fletcher, Charles W. Smith, Joseph J. Perry, Alfred M. Cave, Col. Eli F. Ritter, Edwin P. Hammond and John C. Livezey.

Throughout the succeeding periods of our history Methodism has contributed her share of statesmen and thinkers. Methodism has been in the forefront of every reform, and few indeed are the great reformatory laws which have not been introduced or supported and forced to passage and then enforced by Methodist leaders. There were many public servants during the next period who gave their allegiance to our Church and among those who were placed in seats of honor we find the names of Hon. Henry S. Lane, Congressman, Governor of Indiana and United States Senator; John S. Thompson, Nathan Butts, Alexander C. Downey, Supreme Court Judge of Indiana, Will Cumback, State Senator and Lieutenant Governor; Edward Eggleston, Charles L. Henry, Felix T. McWhirter, Winfield T. Durbin and J. Frank Hanley, Governors of Indiana; Charles W. Fairbanks, United States Vice-President; Albert J. Beveridge, United States Senator; John E. Iglehart, Joseph N. Tillett and Horace Ellis.

And even yet the list does not end. At the present time one finds Methodists in many places of public responsibility. Methodists, many of them the sons of ministers, help make our laws and aid in their enforcement. Both of our present United States senators are members of our church; several of our congressmen worship at our churches; judges in every court are found who claim allegiance with us and interpret the laws as befits men of God. The list is long, far too long to print, but one must mention the names of Harry L. Crumpacker, John H. Skinner, George K. Denton, Henry W. Marshall, Charles A. Carlisle, Francis B. Winn; the present United States Senators from Indiana, James E. Watson and Arthur R. Robinson; Marvin Campbell, A. A. Charles.

Thus, in public as in private life, the Methodists of the state have done and are doing their full duty as citizens. It is a justification of the church to say that many of these men have served faithfully and well. Human, yes, all human, and perhaps criticizable in some respects, but often true workers in the vineyard of the Master, and ready to rise or fall with the result of his work.

Institutions

••••••••••••

DEPAUW UNIVERSITY
By Henry L. Davis, D.D.

PROGRESS—steady, resistless progress, marks the past quadrennium of Methodism in the Indianapolis Area. But nowhere are her steppings more stately than across the campus and through the halls of learning of old DePauw. Perhaps no one institution in the state has contributed more to the Area's growth than has DePauw University in her gift of sons and daughters who have become leaders in the business of Kingdom building throughout Indiana.

It is with just pride that we note the steady advance of this historic institution during the quadrennium now closing. First, the growth has been material. In four years the endowment has leaped from $3,953,864 to $7,118,376—by which magic figures Edward Rector though dead, yet speaketh. The income during the same period has increased from less than $350,000.00 to $500,000.00.

The teaching staff also shows marked growth. In 1923 there were sixty-two professors and instructors in the college of Liberal Arts; today there are eighty-nine on the same staff. If we include in the list laboratory assistants and music school faculty we would have a grand total of one hundred and twenty-five.

The growing faculty was made necessary by the increase of the student body. The present enrollment is 1,666. The increase has taken place in the face of a higher tuition and an advanced standard of scholastic requirements.

DePauw's best growth in the last as in preceding quadrenniums cannot, however, be stated in material terms: is not to be registered in mere numbers, measured by yardstick or rule, nor weighed in the balances. There are things more important than buildings, endowments, income, size of faculty and student body. Real progress is spiritual. This, too, DePauw has had. It is to be written in the story of the sacrificial service of its faculty;

in the tireless and unselfish labor of such administrators as Murlin, Longden, and Towne; in the wonderful spirit of its student body which, having received a larger freedom has not abused it, but working with administration and faculty, presents to the Indianapolis Area the true conception of Christian education—viz. not a couch on which to lie down, nor a tower from which we look down upon others, nor a fortress to resist them, but an instrument for the glory of God and the service of man. Meanwhile, all of this in the last four years has been hallowed by the sacred memory of Edward Rector, DePauw's greatest benefactor.

EVANSVILLE COLLEGE
By A. E. Craig, D.D.

Evansville College, formerly Moores Hill College, relocated at Evansville, Indiana, in 1919, enrolled 563 regular students in 1924-25 and 140 students in extension classes. The registration for 1926-27 was 662, with 302 students in extra-mural classes. The attendance for the closing year of the quadrennium will be approximately 700, with 500 or more students in extra-mural classes. The college is organized as a College of Liberal Arts with closely articulated departments of Education, Engineering (on the cooperative plan), and Business Administration. Opportunity for the study of music has been afforded through the Evansville School of Music, affiliated with the college; and during the last two years special work leading to a degree has been given in Religious Education. The aim of the administration has been to establish the college firmly and to win recognition for the quality of its work rather than to attract numbers or to add buildings. In addition to necessary increase of equipment from year to year, a special gift of $10,000 has been expended in equipment for Engineering, and one of $5,000 in books for the library. A financial campaign in 1924 in Evansville and the Indiana Conference resulted in subscriptions amounting to $741,036.

In June, 1927, Dr. Alfred F. Hughes, who had led in the relocation project and guided the college through its formative years, resigned to accept the presidency of Hamline University. The Board of Trustees acted promptly in choosing a successor, electing to the position Rev. Earl Enyeart Harper, of Auburndale, Mass.

McKENDREE COLLEGE

By Cameron Harmon, D.D., President.

At the beginning of this quadrennium, the college attendance in McKendree was 125. The present year it will run fully 280, and this last figure does not include the music nor other special students nor the summer attendance. The total enrollment with specials for the year will exceed 400 as compared to the 125 four years ago. At that time our outstanding indebtedness totaled $161,500, and our endowment $143,500.

During the quadrennium, the following improvements have been made: permanent equipment in the department of science to the extent of $4,000; in the department of music, $3,400; for athletic field and gymnasium improvements, $13,000; remodeling of president's home and concrete walks, $3,900; new furnace and furnace room, $2,700; Kelvinator and softener for the water, $1,700; library equipment, not including about $1,000 per year for books, $2,000; reseating of chapel, $1,800; new furniture, $500; sundry other permanent improvements such as metal files, etc., $1,000; giving a total expense of $35,000, not including papering, painting, and general overhauling of the plant.

Our endowment fund has increased to $360,000, and this does not include $50,000 recently left us by Judge Gary which we will receive upon the settlement of his estate; $50,000 left in trust by Dr. Hypes; $5,000 from the estate of Senator McKinley; $3,000 from the estate of Dr. James, former President of Illinois University; $12,800 cash bonus which we are to receive within a few days from oil land in California; and many similar amounts which we have received on the annuity plan, as well as an estate of $60,000 which was recently willed to us and the will left in our hands.

Our conference has also provided for us a sustentation fund which, added to our support from the Board of Education, gives

an annual income of $14,000. Although our annual budget has
been increased, yet we are able to strike a balance showing no
deficit.

Our faculty has been greatly strengthened, and the head of
each department has completed at least two years of graduate
work and a two-thirds majority of them the Ph.D. degree or its
equivalent.

We are now in the midst of our 100th consecutive year without
a single break, and we are forced to confess that "The first one
hundred years are the hardest," for the future looks bright, indeed.

During the present year, outstanding speakers came to us on
each Tuesday, bringing an inspirational address to our student
body. We have had with us Branch Rickey of St. Louis; Senator
Williams of the same city; Congressman Upshaw of Alabama;
Dr. E. G. Cutshall of Denver, Colorado; Judge Watson of Mount
Vernon; and many others who have brought helpful and inspiring addresses.

TAYLOR UNIVERSITY

By William B. Freeland, D.D.

The first session of the North Indiana Annual Conference, as
now constituted, met at Fort Wayne, September 22, 1852. It approved the work of the "Fort Wayne Female College," and authorized the founding of a "college for males." The report of the
Conference in 1856 showed that the Female College and the "Collegiate Institute" had been placed under the management of the
same board of trustees. For many years the committee on education continued to report that there was success in the "literary
work" of the college, but that it was hampered by the lack of
adequate financial support.

Thirty-four years later, the North Indiana Conference, assembled in Muncie, received from the committee on education
the following report. "This institution has had a struggle for
many years. There is now an indebtedness of twenty thousand
dollars. We recommend that the College be sold, and the surplus

HOLDEN
HOSPITAL
CARBONDALE
ILLINOIS

NEW UNIT
METHODIST
HOSPITAL
INDIANAPOLIS

NURSES HOME
INDIANAPOLIS

NURSES HOME
GARY HOSPITAL

NEW HOSPITAL BUILDINGS

proceeds be used for buildings in a new location." The trustees were so instructed, and at the following session reported that sale had been made to "Taylor University." After the work of one year, the citizens of Upland offered a tract of ten acres at that place, and this new organization, which called the school by the name of the great missionary, William Taylor, moved the institution to Upland, and erected the H. Maria Wright Hall, in the summer of 1893. Taylor University has followed a consistent building program. The most notable accomplishments have been Music Hall and the large and beautiful woman's dormitory, which rivals the best buildings of this kind in the middle west.

Under the new organization, the Reverend Thaddeus C. Reade, D.D., became the first president, and gave unselfish service to the enterprise. He was followed by the Reverend C. W. Winchester, D.D., who continued the policies of Doctor Reade. For eight years, the Reverend Monroe Vayhinger, D.D., performed heroic service as the president. James M. Taylor, who followed, resigned, and was succeeded by the present president, the Reverend John Paul, D.D. Doctor Paul, who is a member of the North Indiana Conference, has been very successful. Under his guiding hand financial policies have been established, confidence promoted, and a gradual but substantial growth sustained.

Taylor University is inter-denominational in its work and form of government. It was under the patronage of the National Association of Local Preachers for a quarter of a century; but now there is a duly organized Legal Hundred, which is the foundation society of the school. A majority of the members of this body must be members of the Methodist Episcopal Church. The prudential management is carried on by a board of nine trustees, who are selected by the larger body.

The instruction in this unique institution includes not only the courses in liberal arts, but also work in theology, music, expression, and pedagogy. Many students from distant states and countries have sought equipment for the work of life, and returned to render efficient service. The standards of instruction have been advanced, and the institution is given standard rating by the State of Indiana. There is confident expectation of the continued progress of Taylor University.

THE WESLEY FOUNDATIONS

By H. D. Bollinger, Minister for Students, Purdue University.

John Wesley was more interested in a condition than a theory. His life consisted of a series of changes brought about by a continuous effort to meet the emergencies that arose in the presence of human necessities. This is also true of Methodism. She is quick to adapt herself. In the presence of pressing social, political and religious problems, Methodism has not formulated new creeds or doctrines but has adapted her machinery. An illustration of this fact is the way in which Christian experience is articulated in our far-reaching program of religious education. In this great movement Methodism is conserving her distinctive idealism, the evangelistic emphasis.

Wesley Foundation work is one of the newest and yet one of the most important factors in the movement of religious education. It is born of a necessity and is Methodism's answer to a real need. Historically, we have fostered our own denominational colleges. The gigantic post war trek of youth into the halls of learning filled not only these institutions but the state universities as well. This has presented a peculiar problem in Indiana for we have more Methodist young people in our state universities than the total number of students enrolled in the Methodist colleges of the state. What shall be done with these young people? Shall they have any constructive religious training while in the state university? The Wesley Foundations of the state are answers to these questions.

What is a Wesley Foundation? Briefly, it is an institution wherein is conducted a program that seeks to conserve, interpret, and articulate Christian idealism. A Wesley Foundation has an incorporated body of men, who, like the trustees of a church, are responsible for the work that is done. The actual conduct of the program is in the hands of a student cabinet comparable to the official board of a church. The motto of the work is, "of the students, by the students, and for the students." The pastor of the church in which the work centers is the Director of the Foundation and working with him is the Minister for Students. A social and religious center is maintained furnishing for the students "a home away from home." At the Wesley Foundation at Purdue a house calendar is maintained and hundreds of students use the house during the school year. In addition to the regular Wesley Foundation organizations, nine different student organizations use the building as a regular meeting place, including the Dames Club (wives of married students), the Chinese Club, and the Filipino Club. As soon as students register their religious affiliation or preference at the University the Wesley Foundation workers focus their attention upon them in the effort to provide for them a worthwhile program of religious education. A brief glance at the Wesley Foundation schedule at Purdue University serves to indicate how this is done. Two morning watch services are held each week on Tuesdays and Thursdays. A different leader is provided for each one of these meetings of prayer and consecration. A class in religious education taught by the minister for students is held every Thursday evening. A social is held each Friday evening wherein students can have a wholesome recreational time under ideal conditions. Two student orchestras and a sixty voice choir not only provide music for the Sunday program but also on special occasions and for out of town concerts. Religious extension teams hold services in nearby churches and a social service group holds meetings every two weeks at institutions in the community. Sunday classes in religious education provide the opportunity for laboratory work in religion and of course the regular worship services of the church seek to stimulate a creative Christian response in the hearts and lives of the young people. One of the most important phases of the work is the contacts made with students from other lands. Most of them are keen minded graduates of foreign universities who attend our state universities for graduate study. Realizing the strategic missionary opportunity of a personal association, a special effort is made to interest them in the Christian program. An example of the effectiveness of this type of work was in the case of a Chinese student who entered Purdue University for graduate work in railroad engineering. He was a Confucianist and enrolled in the class in the comparative study of religion where an attempt was made to make a fair minded study of all religions. Not long after he offered his first prayer in the morning watch prayer service and a few days later became a Christian. He returned to China fired with the Christian ideal and has since become one of the leading engineers of the Chinese nationalist government in the standardization of the different guage railroads of his native country. Similar work along all these lines of personal consecration, worship, social service, religious extension, recreation, music, pageantry, and religious education is carried on by the Wesley Foundation at Indiana University.

A Wesley Foundation is an institution of religious conservation. This does not mean, of course, an institution of religious conservatism. It is not designed to perpetuate outworn forms of creed or conduct. However, if the machinery of religious training in the church and church school has awakened or developed anything of value in the life of a young person, it is worth conserving while that individual is in a wideawake atmosphere of university life. The machinery of a Wesley Foundation is geared to the program of the local church. The work in each instance, according to the general policy of Methodism, centers in the Methodist church that is closest to the campus of the state university. In Indiana these churches are First Church, Bloomington, and First Church, West Lafayette. All of the normal activities that a local church carries on are conducted in these churches with a view to making the student familiar with church life. Already these Wesley Foundations have turned back into Indiana churches large numbers of alert, consecrated young people with a desire to serve.

Furthermore, Wesley Foundations are personnel agencies of religion. They seek to help students to "find" themselves. The sudden change from the environs of the home and home community into the kaleidoscopic atmosphere of the university, where demands are made on the student's time, interests and energy, throws many of them into utter confusion. In such a situation, the Wesley Foundation, with the warmth of its social-fellowship program, seeks to orientate the student. Throughout his university career, the Wesley Foundation is the student's personal friend seeking to guide him into the vocation wherein he will be of most service to his fellowman.

A Wesley Foundation is an agency to stimulate the desire on the part of youth ethically to interpret Jesus in the social order. Discussion groups, classes in religious education, quest groups in the philosophy of life and living, are fostered by these institutions for that purpose. The net result is not only ministers and missionaries but also consecrated lay graduates who are adventurers in the serious business of attempting to live like Jesus in our complex social order.

There are two incorporated Wesley Foundations in our state, the one at Indiana and the one at Purdue. In addition, there are two soon to be formed, one at the Muncie Normal and one at the Indiana State Normal at Terre Haute. The Foundation at Indiana University is supported by the Indiana Conference while the Foundation at Purdue University draws its suport from the North Indiana and Northwest Indiana Conferences. There is a movement on foot by representatives of the three conferences and the four state schools to formulate a merger wherein there would be a single statewide Wesley Foundation request for annual funds and special appeals. It is to be hoped that such a merger will be completed. In the meantime, the much appreciated help now given will continue to be disbursed as wisely as possible by the directors and workers who are constantly conscious of the fact that deficiencies now existing will some day be overcome. The incorporated Foundations at Indiana and Purdue are rendering inadequate service for they are in dire need of proper equipment and a larger staff of workers. The facts show that both universities are growing. Some statistical information is very interesting:

	INDIANA	PURDUE
Enrollment ten years ago	2659	1844
(Total annual enrollment)		
Methodist students ten years ago	850	557
Enrollment five years ago	4837	3360
Methodist students five years ago	1625	955
Enrollment today (First Semester 1927-1928)	3424	3647
Methodist students (First Semester 1927-1928)	1030	1203
Value of new buildings erected on or near the campus during the past five years	$1,650,000	$1,945,417
Amount the state spends per year per student	$300	$400
Amount the Methodist Church spends per year per student	$2	$5

These figures clearly indicate Indiana Methodism's challenge. If we are serious about the youth problem, if we mean business when we talk of realistically interpreting Jesus, then the high hour is here. Something will soon be done and the church, the institution of the heart, will arise and match the program of the state in the university, the institution of the head. When that day arrives, there will be a noticeable difference in the moral and ethical life of the new generation.

METHODIST HOSPITAL WORK IN THE INDIANAPOLIS AREA

By John W. McFall, D.D.

Indiana Methodism has hospitals located at Indianapolis, Princeton, Ft. Wayne and Gary. The total value of these institutions, including ground, buildings and equipment is approximately $2,275,000.00. They represent an important business, dealing not in the necessities of life, but with life itself. They are not owned and operated for financial gain, but seek the higher good, that of healing the sick in the name of Christ.

During the past quadrennium these hospitals have made marked progress. Last year 12,224 patients were admitted to the Indianapolis hospital, the largest number ever admitted in one year. For the same period of time there were 8,882 surgical cases cared for, 527 more than the previous year. More than $101,-000.00 in free service was given last year, which means $276.00 per day or $11.50 per hour for the entire year. The other three hospitals of the state are doing proportionately as well.

The hospital management in ministering to the physical welfare of the patients is also mindful of their spiritual needs. For all the patients the services of a minister of the Gospel are available on request. A friendly Christian atmosphere pervades the sick rooms and corridors of these homes of healing. No one who comes into these institutions is permitted to overlook the fact that these are Christian organizations supported by the Church. No hospital cases are therefore turned away for any reason other than for the lack of room. The services of the most skilled surgeons and physicians are available to rich and poor alike.

From a financial consideration our hospitals are a liability upon the church, but humanely and spiritually they are a tremendous asset. They exist for service, and the value of the service rendered is measured by the intelligence, skill and high Christian ideals of the physicians on the hospital staff, the nurses in service and training, and the hospital management. They practice the healing ministry of our Lord, and give to the communities in which they are located, and to the state as well, a sense of security, for no one can tell when he may need their service. Their helping and healing ministry is well known all over this state.

Extensive material improvements have been made this quadrennium in all our hospitals. At Gary a new and modern nurses' home has been erected at a cost of $90,000.00. It will provide homes for the student nurses for many years to come. At Indianapolis a new nurses' home is nearing completion, costing $600,000. It will comfortably house 300 student nurses with rest and reading rooms provided. A new heating and power plant has been completed, with laundry equipment costing $198,000. At Princeton a new laundry has been installed. Lots adjacent to the Ft. Wayne hospital have been purchased with a view to enlarging the present building. A new unit is being added to the Indianapolis hospital to meet the demands for increased hospital service. It will be eight stories high, with walls heavy enough to carry eight more stories to be added later. It will be modern in every particular. Eminent physicians and surgeons have given the local building committee valuable aid in planning for this new unit.

The four hospitals are incorporated under the name of the Methodist Episcopal Hospital and Deaconness Home of the State of Indiana. Arthur V. Brown is president of the board of trustees of the corporation. The Reverend George M. Smith, D.D., is the general superintendent. On the board of trustees are men and women who are ever loyal to the best interests of these institutions of healing. The executive committee meets monthly and is made up of a group of men who give unstintedly of their time and strength to the hospitals that belong to Indiana Methodism.

Within the Indianapolis Area we have also the Holden Hospital, located at Carbondale, Illinois. During the past quadrennium a new addition has been added, increasing the capacity to fifty beds. The building, grounds and equipment reach a valuation of approximately $200,000.

In 1927 Mrs. Carrie Holden gave to this institution six hundred acres of land located in central Kansas. This is considered one of the largest gifts ever given to a Methodist institution in southern Illinois.

The hospital is governed by a conference board of twenty-six members. Thirteen of the members are appointed by the conference and thirteen by the Women's Home Missionary Society. Dr. J. S. Cummins is president of the conference board, Mrs. Adella B. Mitchell, of Carbondale, is chairman of the board of directors, and A. R. Pengilly is superintendent of the hospital.

ORPHANS' AND CHILDREN'S HOMES OF THE INDIANAPOLIS AREA.

By C. C. Hall, D.D.

Two orphanages are operating at the present time in the Area, and one is in the process of organization, to-wit:—

I. The Bashor Orphanage.

The Bashor Deaconess Orphanage Association holds one farm of one hundred and fifty-nine acres and another plot of ground of thirty-seven and one-half acres near the city of Goshen, Indiana, also nearly $5,000 in money. The land was given several years ago by Mr. and Mrs. Bashor to found an orphanage. A board of trustees holds the property for the North Indiana Conference.

II. The Indiana Methodist Episcopal Children's Home.

This home was moved from Greencastle to Lebanon, Indiana, in August, 1924, and is under the direction of the Indiana and Northwest Indiana Conferences. Part of this property was donated by the citizens of Lebanon. Additional ground was purchased by the trustees, ten acres in the tract, five acres in native forest trees.

The plan calls for four buildings—an administration building, a service building and two cottage halls. In August, 1926 the foundations for the Amanda C. Swift Memorial Hall and a service building were laid, and in September, 1927 both of the buildings were dedicated.

The Swift Memorial Hall has a capacity for thirty-five children. The two buildings and the site cost $63,000. The children in this home attend the public school and the local church. The children are placed in approved homes. Rev. Joseph L. Stout is the efficient superintendent and renders valuable service in caring for the homeless children of this conference.

MEMORIAL
HOME
FOR THE AGED
WARREN
INDIANA

METHODIST
ORPHANAGE
MT. VERNON
ILLINOIS

THE
METHODIST
CHILDREN'S
HOME
OF INDIANA

OLD FOLK'S
HOME
LAWRENCEVILLE
ILLINOIS

CENTERS OF CHRISTIAN CARE

III. The Orphans' and Children's Home of the Southern Illinois Conference.

The work of caring for homeless children by the Southern Illinois Conference was inaugurated September, 1911. The Home was formally opened at Creal Springs, Illinois, in 1913. After a few years a fire destroyed one building, and a more central location was sought. Twenty-five acres of ground with a large brick dwelling in the northwest corner of Mt. Vernon was purchased in 1921. A large fireproof building was dedicated September, 1924, with a capacity for fifty-six children besides caretakers. We have property values around $90,000. We have an average of fifty children. This is also a receiving home. Children are placed in approved homes. Children attend public school and local church. Another building is in contemplation. There are no debts. C. C. Hall is the superintendent.

HOMES FOR THE AGED.

By B. S. Hollopeter, D.D.

Two homes for the aged are operated under the auspices of the Methodist Episcopal Church within the bounds of the Indianapolis Area. One is conducted at Warren, Indiana, under the patronage of the North Indiana Conference. The other is located at Lawrenceville, Illinois, and is under the control of the Southern Illinois Conference.

The Old People's Home at Warren, Indiana, came into existence in 1910 as the result of a gift of $65,000 from William and Ruth C. Chopson. The North Indiana Conference raised an additional $25,000 to meet the conditions of this gift and the home was established. During the eighteen years of its existence many other large gifts have been received, bringing the present assets of the home up to $406,000 with no indebtedness. During its history 248 worthy old people have enjoyed its shelter and care. Now 109 are living in it.

The home is managed by a board of trustees elected by the North Indiana Conference, but its benefits are not confined to those who live within the bounds of that conference. The present board of trustees is composed of the following ministers and laymen who give their time and talent to the management without remuneration: Rev. C. U. Wade, Muncie; Rev. B. S. Hollopeter, Huntington; Rev. W. W. Wiant, Fort Wayne, Rev. B. M. Bechdolt, Garrett; Rev. Leroy W. Kemper, Newcastle; Rev. F.A. Hall, Anderson; M. B. Stultz, Huntington; Arthur H. Sapp, Huntington; C. W. Beecher, Peru; Lloyd M. Cline, Bluffton; O. A. Pulley, Warren. The superintendent is A. W. Clark, and the matron is Miss Myrta M. Clark. The corresponding secretary is B. S. Hollopeter, who has general oversight of all matters pertaining to the institution.

Last year an $8,000 dairy barn was built. This year a frigidaire system, a water softener, and dairy equipment have been added. The entire interior of the home has been painted, the floors polished, and many other improvements made.

An excellent home spirit is maintained and the devotional element is faithfully emphasized. The family prayer hour observed each morning in the chapel is a real spiritual uplift to the members of the home.

The Old Folk's Home at Lawrenceville, Illinois, is under the superintendency of the Rev. Charles L. Coleman of the Southern Illinois Conference, and the management of a board of ministers and laymen authorized by that conference.

The most significant fact concerning the history of this institution during the quadrennium has been its removal and rebuilding. Formerly located at St. Francesville, under the superintendency of the late Mr. J. B. Stout, this home increased in its service until it was necessary to find other facilities. A private dwelling in Edwardsville, the home of Miss Addie Snell, was offered for the use of the home and became an adjunct to the work at St. Francesville.

In the meantime plans were under way for the building of a new structure in a more suitable location where all modern conveniences were available. Upon the invitation of the city of Lawrenceville, together with the present of a very desirable site by the business men of the city, the new home was located at that place. The new building and equipment cost a little more than $135,000. The grounds given by the people of the city represented a value of $6,000. Additional gifts brought the total value of the plant up to $150,000 with a rated capacity of fifty-four persons. The service of the home is expanding with the facilities made possible by additional funds and in the near future it is expected to be operating at full capacity.

Our Earliest Shrine

••••••••••

THE FIRST METHODIST EPISCOPAL CHURCH
OF INDIANA

ON THURSDAY, September 10, 1925, the following program was rendered in connection with the relocation of the tiny log First Methodist Church building of Indiana, and the dedication of the permanent grounds at Charlestown. This event also celebrated the One Hundredth Anniversary of the assembling of the second session of the Illinois Conference, the first to be held within the bounds of Indiana, on August 25, 1825.

At 3:00 o'clock in the afternoon the Indiana Conference, representatives of the conferences of Indianapolis Area, and citizens assembled at the Old Church, Bishop Frederick D. Leete, presiding.

The hymn, "Faith of Our Fathers," was announced by E. H. Wood, D.D., retired minister, son of a veteran of this conference and nephew of Aaron Wood, a member of the Illinois Conference in 1825.

The Scripture was read by John Alexander Hayes, great great grandson of Reverend James Garner, who preached the Christmas sermon in this old log church in the year 1813. He read from James Garner's Bible the same lesson used at that service.

PRAYER BY E. A. ROBERTSON, D.D.

E. A. Robertson, Barth Place, Indianapolis, great grandson of Nathan Robertson, builder of the old log church, who was believed to have been the first Methodist in Indiana, led in prayer as follows:

Almighty and ever-living GOD, most merciful and gracious: We love Thee and would worship Thee always through Christ whom we yearn to serve with unwavering fidelity and unflagging devotion. We love to worship Thee, O Holy Ghost, with whom each day is Pentecost, each night Nativity, and for aye our risen Lord were lost but for Thy company.

May we walk with GOD as did our fathers who traveled a trackless wilderness on the high mission of spreading Scriptural holiness in every settlement and throughout our Methodist societies.

May this memorial hour be to us, not so much a meditation by the grave-side of departed Christian warriors who have long since laid their armor down, having fought the fight of faith, as a receiving upon our uplifted faces the light that shone on land and sea, the light from the transfigured face of the White Comrade, even the Captain of the Lord's hosts, as HE leads us from conquering to conquest.

May all our work, as individuals and as a strong conference, the virtual successor of the historic conference which was in session at about this time of the year, one hundred years ago, be begun, continued and ended in Thee, O Thou Master of Assemblies!

We thank Thee for the good examples of those adventurous "circuit-riders" who rode on horseback over these very grounds, by blazed trees or along cowpaths or deer-trails, and through swollen streams, sleeping at night under the open stars, enduring hardships with apostolic zeal and daring, worthy a place in GOD'S Hall of Fame.

We pray that the mantle of their courage, their vision, their evangelistic fervency and power may fall upon us, the prophets of the New Day.

We beseech Thee, O Thou great Head of the Church, that in these times of vacillating opinion, of unholy religious controversy, of unsettled faith, of lowering moral standards and of formality of worship and religious life, that our people may cling with renewed loyalty and consecration to the faith of our fathers,—a living faith because energized by the indwelling of the Holy Spirit. May the daily life of all of us be so sanctified through His cleansing, as to be more courageous, invigorating, thoughtful, winsome and more useful.

May we so incarnate Christian militancy that we shall face organized evil, now so intrenched in politics, with the same courage with which the fathers faced the arrow and tomahawk of the Indian or made a stand against the bear!

We bless Thy name, O Lord, that we are comforted and

heartened in the thought that there are still in all our fields of labor, both at home and abroad, many infallible proofs that the heroic and sacrificial spirit of the fathers has not utterly died, but the memories of these early pioneers still inspire and embolden to deeds noble and imperishable.

And now we humbly pray that a "double portion of the Elijahan spirit may fall upon us" that there may be such a rebirth of the simple, fervent, Pauline type of Christian faith and life that, throughout our borders, we may know the joy, exemplify the power and proclaim with hearts inflamed of the Holy Spirit our distinctive message of a free, a full and a felt salvation.

We, the representatives of Indiana state-wide Methodism of the present day gladly acknowledge our debt of gratitude to the early fathers who planted our Church in these parts at the very beginning of our national existence, and may God forbid that the memory of their glorious deeds should ever perish from our people.

Hear us, Thou God of our fathers, as now and here, we their children, by the office and ministry of our chief pastor, solemnly and gratefully rededicate this relocated Bethel Methodist meeting house, as a hallowed shrine, about which shall cluster for years to come the tenderest and most inspiring memories.

And now, let Thy blessing be upon us. Keep us from the ignoble, whether in thought or imagination or friendship or in official relation. Be Thou our sky of hope, of morning, when it is black night, starless and void. Be Thou our sun and shield so that we shall not stumble and that at night it shall be light!

We humbly implore the continuous presence of Thy Holy Spirit by whose abiding we sometimes sob and sometimes sing,— "ABBA, ABBA FATHER."

Whenever our tired hands fall and we can no longer work, grant us to be among that elect company whose Christ-like works do follow them.

Receive our oblation in the name of GOD our Father, Jesus our Redeemer and the Holy Spirit our Comforter, and may the very GOD of Peace sanctify us wholly and make us faithful ministers of the New Testament, sending to all nations the blessed Gospel of God and so fulfill through us Thy purpose for the world's evangelization; and at last, when our work is done,— when the hour comes when it shall be said to each one of us: "Give an account of thy stewardship; for thou must be no longer steward," —bring us to the reward, and to reunion with our departed fathers, for the sake of Jesus Christ our adorable Saviour!— AMEN.

The hymn, "I Love Thy Kingdom, Lord" was announced by Virgil E. Rorer, D.D., pastor Meridian Street Church, Indianapolis.

Historical Statement by Reverend J. E. Murr, D.D.

A brief historical statement was made by J. Edward Murr, Superintendent of New Albany District, Indiana Conference, as follows:

The Methodist movement under Wesley was the spiritual development of the great Reformation, and in consequence made for the renaissance of religion just as the Renaissance had made for the revival of letters and art.

Notwithstanding the fact that Methodism was conceived in the Established Church and born of Anglican parentage in England's greatest university, yet the new movement was regarded as an ecclesiastical foundling, receiving in consequence no official recognition whatever. Thus in this crisis God thrust the Methodists out to raise up a holy people with the unmistakable purpose of spreading scriptural holiness throughout the Parish of the World.

Since Methodism was not founded upon a negation, but a positive declaration of purpose to restore that which was lost, its creed (if creed it has) may be found in the emphasis upon the original primitive Christian principles of justification, regeneration, sanctification, and the witness of the Spirit.

The new movement did not relish the slight visited upon it by the Establishment's failure to give it official recognition, but Wesley and his associates did not for that reason turn aside from their divine calling and objective, and thus make the ecclesiastical mistake of indulging in disputation over non-essentials, such as the fabulous doctrine of apostolic succession and other purely extraneous matters.

Methodism, true to its origin and in keeping with its positive declarations, justified itself in history by giving to England her greatest administrator and ecclesiastical statesman, her foremost hymn-writer of the age, and the greatest pulpit orator of all time.

Methodism from the beginning has refused to be interested in the doctrine of apostolic succession, realizing that a Church or Establishment that claims the succession because it is the true Church, cannot at the same time properly assert that it is the true Church because it has the succession.

The new movement at the first and until this present time, has been quite properly concerned as to its place in the apostolic procession, and in the light of history, this is reasonably satisfactory.

With a zeal surpassing that of the Jesuits, and with an apostolic faith in the confident assurance of providential oversight and direction, Methodist itinerants, early in the eighteenth century, joined the Old World emigrant train to America, and when the vast empire west of the Alleghenies was being settled, representatives of the Methodist movement came to this Ohio Valley, and by indefatigable labors and unexampled spirit and zeal, under an ecclesiastical system peculiarly adapted to the formative and constructive period of American life, they saved civilization to the future republic as well as to Christianity itself, leading a large portion of the citizenship peopling this western wilderness—a people who were in great danger of lapsing into barbarism.

The apostolic Asbury and his associates blazed trails through the western wilds, and as early as the year 1797, the Kentucky District with William McKendree as presiding elder, numbered 1672 Methodist members.

In the year 1799 Nathan Robertson, the first Methodist in this State, and one of a Methodist family of five brothers, emigrated from Kentucky to a place some three miles distant from the present village of Charlestown, located in Clark County, Indiana.

At a quarterly meeting held by William McKendree in the year 1800 on the Hinkstone Circuit in Kentucky, a revival of unusual power was experienced. Among the converts of that meeting were two young men—Samuel Parker and Edward Talbott, both of whom had much to do with introducing Methodism in Indiana. Parker had been given exhorter's license by McKendree, and with characteristic zeal he crossed the Ohio River and appeared in what was known as the Springville settlement. After visiting from house to house, he was subsequently joined by Talbott, and the two conducted a revival of two days' duration in the village of Springville. This town has long since disappeared, and the original site is now included in a farm owned by a Mr. Fletcher Ross. Yet this village became historic on two accounts. First, it marked the beginnings of Methodism in Indiana, and also became the first county seat of Clark County, and therefore, the second seat of government in the state.

While at Springville, Parker met Nathan Robertson, as well as Mr. Gazaway, Prather and Jacobs, each one representing what may quite properly be called a neighborhood or settlement. All were members of the Methodist Church.

On his return to Kentucky, Parker reported the results of his missionary tour to McKendree, and the future Bishop came in person to this general community in Indiana in the year Eighteen Hundred and One. He crossed the Ohio in a "Jo Boat," above what is known as Charlestown Landing. The presumption is in favor of a previous understanding with some of the pioneer settlers, since a Mr. Robinet who furnished the boat and served as McKendree's guide was a resident of the immediate neighborhood of Mr. Gazaway. The Gazaway home was not far from the present location of the Salem church.

Here at Gazaway's cabin McKendree preached on the evening of the day of his arrival. Nathan Robertson and others were present at this service. On the invitation of Nathan Robertson, McKendree preached on the following morning in his home, and on the evening of that same day he conducted service at Prather's. The next day, McKendree re-crossed the Ohio at the falls, preaching the first sermon ever delivered by a Methodist preacher in the city of Louisville.

Classes had been organized at Gazaway's, Robertson's and Prather's, with the assurance that these points would be regularly served by the pastor of Salt River and Shelby Circuit. Accordingly, Benjamin Lakin, the circuit rider, came soon after McKendree's visit. This was in the year 1801.

A log church 20x18 feet was erected at Gazaway's during the late autumn of the year 1804, but unfortunately it was accidentally burned before it had been roofed and floored.

In the year 1807, this old log church called Bethel Meeting-house was built on a slight elevation some three hundred yards distant from the residence of Nathan Robertson.

At about the same distance from this old church there stood also a pioneer fort to which the citizens of the general community would flee for safety during Indian uprisings. We have a record of at least one such siege, but the citizens were not harmed, and the fort and the old church escaped the firebrand.

There was no provision made for the heating of Bethel meeting house, and pioneer ingenuity resorted to the happy expedient of burning a log-heap the day prior to the preaching service, in order to obtain a bed of live coals which were placed in large iron kettles, and carried into the church. The building was well chinked and daubed, and thus this bottled-up heat over night insured some degree of comfort for the worshippers.

About the same time that Bethel Church was erected, the class at Prather's also built a log meeting-house called Jacob's Chapel. In view of the fact, this community has always maintained a house of worship from that day to this, and at the present time has a successor to the original Jacob's Chapel. There is therefore a peculiar historic distinction rightfully belonging to Jacob's or Prather's, that does not obtain at Robertson's. The same may also be said of Gazaway's, with Salem as its successor.

There appears to be a mistaken apprehension relative to the formation of Silver Creek Circuit—more particularly as to its size. Silver Creek Circuit at one time included all the settlements from Mt. Vernon near the Illinois state line up as far as Madison and reaching back from the Ohio River to a considerable distance inland.

In the year 1807, Moses Ashworth was assigned as preacher in charge of this new circuit and in the autumn of the year 1808, under his leadership, was held the first camp-meeting ever conducted in the state. This camp-ground was in a maple grove surrounding Old Bethel Church, and on the farm of Nathan Robertson. This camp-ground became a noted gathering place of the pioneer Methodists. Here it was in the year 1809 that George Knight Hester, to use his own words, "got religion under Sela Paine." He subsequently became an itinerant Methodist preacher —was the father of four Methodist preachers, as well as also the grandfather of a number of Methodist preachers, and it was Hester and his remarkable wife, "Aunt Bena," who were so largely responsible for giving to Methodism the six Methodist preachers from the Bovard family.

One of the curious, not to say pathetic, incidents transpiring in Indiana Methodist history has to do with this same Moses Ashworth, the first pastor of the first circuit in Indiana. There was a native prejudice existing among both preachers and laymen in that early period against a married preacher who yet continued to belong to the traveling connection. William Burke was the first married preacher west of the Alleghenies, who continued to travel. Ashworth married in 1813, and in view of this prejudice, asked for and was granted a location. In the year 1832, when the Indiana Conference met in its first session in the city of New Albany, Ashworth requested to be restored to the effective relation, but his request was refused.

Methodism of Indiana owes a debt of gratitude to the memory of Moses Ashworth, that has never as yet been paid. His ashes rest in a more or less neglected grave near Mt. Vernon, Indiana.

In the year 1813, James Garner, the preacher in charge of Silver Creek Circuit, preached the first Christmas sermon ever delivered by a Methodist preacher in the state. The place was in the pulpit of Bethel Church. His text was: "We have seen His star in the East, and have come to worship Him."

The log church has had a varied career, since it has been rebuilt four times. Erected in 1807, it served as a preaching place for thirty years, and in the year 1837, by reason of the death of Nathan Robertson and the consequent changes in ownership of land, the old meeting-house was removed to the farm of James Robertson.

In its new location which was about one-fourth of a mile south from the first location, it served for twenty years more, and in the year 1857 it was abandoned, since the church in Charlestown was more central and more commodious.

For a number of years the old church was used as a sheep barn. One cannot escape the thought that there was at least beautiful appropriateness in thus shepherding the flocks by night.

Later, the old structure was once more removed near Lexington highway, and in the year 1903, in obedience to an order of the Indiana Conference, the writer (J. Edward Murr) purchased the building for the sum of $50.00, and rebuilt it on the original foundation where the pioneer fathers had placed it in 1807.

In July of this present year, 1925, a committee composed of Bishop Frederick D. Leete, J. Edward Murr, and Joseph Morrow, who had been selected and authorized by the Indiana State Council of the Methodist Episcopal Church to purchase a suitable site for the old log church, thus once again removed the historic building to its present location in Charlestown.

The logs composing the present structure are the original ones throughout, without any alterations in the building as to dimensions or openings, such as windows and doors, save that the plates had to be replaced, and in two instances logs had decayed beyond the possibility of further use.

By a rather strange coincidence, in the year Nineteen Hundred Three, when we were preparing to rebuild the old church, on its original site, the Nathan Robertson barn was being dismantled and with some degree of appropriateness I substituted oak logs from the Nathan Robertson barn. These may be easily distinguished since the original building was of yellow poplar, save one log of black walnut. The opening in the north side for a stove-pipe belongs to the period when the building ceased to be used as a church, and was experiencing its many changes.

Stoves came to this western country in Eighteen Hundred Nineteen, and the first one made in the Ohio Valley was fashioned by a gentleman whose home was in Charlestown—Allen Barnett.

Indiana Methodism today is more particularly celebrating the centennial of annual conferences, since the Illinois Conference convened here in Charlestown, August 25, 1825. However, we must not lose sight of the fact that prior to 1825, Indiana Methodism belonged to the Missouri Conference, which had been created by the General Conference session of 1816.

The Missouri Conference included the present states of Arkansas, Missouri, Illinois and Indiana, and in the year of 1817, the Missouri Annual Conference held its annual session in Bethel Church near the present city of Washington, Indiana, thus antedating the Illinois session by eight years.

In the General Conference session of 1824, the Missouri Conference was divided, and Illinois and Indiana with the southern portion of Michigan, constituted what is known as the Illinois Conference. The General Conference of 1824 met in May, and the time was altogether too short for the fixing of time and place elsewhere for the meeting of the new conference, hence it met with the old Missouri Conference at Lookinglass Prairie, Illinois, and was presided over by Bishops Roberts, McKendree and Joshua Soule.

The ecclesiastical historians have failed to ascertain why the name "Illinois" was given to this conference rather than that of Indiana, in view of the larger numerical strength in Indiana. Some of the old pioneer itinerants of that period suggested that the name was a compromise one, a suggestion however that appears to possess but little weight. I venture a suggestion merely. In view of the presence of Peter Cartwright as a member of the eighteen hundred twenty-four General Conference session from Illinois, and his commanding influence, the name thus doubtless was suggested by him. Indiana Methodism never at any time in the past, much less now, has had any occasion to call the matter in question; however, it is quite apparent that Indiana Methodism possessed some considerable advantages over the Illinois brothers, as may be observed in the fact that five of the seven annual sessions of the Illinois Conferences were held in Indiana. The 1825 session at Charlestown; 1826, Bloomington, Indiana; 1827, Edwardsville, Illinois; 1828, Madison, Ind.; 1829, Mt. Carmel, Illinois; 1830, at Vincennes, Indiana, and the last session at Indianapolis, Indiana, 1831.

The Illinois Conference session held at Charlestown, Indiana, August 25, 1825, was presided over by Bishops Roberts and McKendree. There were four districts with thirty-six circuits, twenty-two of which were in Indiana. There were forty-one preachers in attendance.

The business of the conference was transacted in a small room in a brick residence, yet fairly well preserved, which was at that time occupied or owned at least by Rev. James Sharp, an itinerant Methodist preacher who had entered the traveling connection in Carolina in the year 1813. The preaching services during the conference week and on the Sabbath, were held in a grove some fifty yards south of the present B. & O. passenger depot.

In order to more nearly appreciate the historic significance of this centennial of Indiana, Illinois and Michigan Methodism, we but need to be reminded of certain outstanding things which the young generation more particularly must visualize so as to make possible adequate appreciation, and thus be enabled to properly assess religious values.

First of all, when Methodism was introduced in Indiana by Samuel Parker in 1800, there were sixteen hundred twenty-six white members and one hundred fifteen colored in all of this vast Ohio Valley empire, which included Kentucky. We had three hundred seven preachers in the United States and Canada, with a total membership in the new world of 72,874 and 109,961 in Europe, and 13,667 in Nova Scotia, Newfoundland and the West Indies, making a grand total of 196,502 Methodists in the world.

The population of Indiana at that time was 2,973, with Vincennes as the only town, with 1,538 inhabitants. Indianapolis and Corydon—the two future capitols of the State had not been founded and the Indianapolis site was at that time inhabited by Indian tribes.

Moreover, there were no railroads, no bridges, no public highways, and there was not a stone or brick house in the entire state.

Such worthies as Nathan Bangs, Elijah Hedding, Enoch George, Emery and Joshua Soule, were just entering the Methodist ministry. Every one of the forty-one preachers who attended this 1825 session reached Charlestown on horseback. Every preacher save McKendree was dressed either in homespun or leather. The regulation dress was round breasted coat, low vest with corners cut off, short breeches and long stockings.

The itinerant had a custom of combing the hair straight back, cutting it short from the forehead to midway on the crown, and since he suffered it to grow long, it fell about his neck and shoulders.

McKendree was distinguished by his dress, since he wore a high rolling collar with a coat of blue color, which possessed unusual length, with brass buttons much in evidence, and since the tail of the coat ran out to a sharp point, there is small wonder that his dress would be remembered.

Samuel Parker, who introduced Methodism in Indiana, was a tall slim awkward man with large blue eyes, and possessed an exceedingly large Roman nose. When he preached, the inside of his upper lip protruded ungracefully. Moreover, he had a long sharp chin which he turned to a good advantage, particularly in cold weather, using this member to hold up the blanket which he wore in lieu of an overcoat. In the center of the blanket he had cut a hole, which to prevent it from raveling, was securely bound. Through this hole Parker would push his rather smallish head and allowing the blanket to rest upon the point of the chin, he rode forth, bidding defiance to wind and rain.

There was not a college graduate among the entire group, yet we must not for that reason form an improper estimate of these pioneers. In the best sense of that term, many of them were truly educated, and perhaps one-third of them were pulpit orators, the equal of the best in our time. Then, too, some of these men were possessed of great administrative ability and ecclesiastical foresight, quite the equal of our wisest men of today. It would have been worth the making of a long journey for any of us today to have been privileged to hear a single sermon of any one of these men.

Perhaps there is peculiar appropriateness just here to introduce an excerpt from a sermon preached by John Strange, who was present at this conference of Eighteen Hundred Twenty-five. It has always been said of him that he was the most widely known and best loved Methodist preacher that Indiana has ever produced.

"My alma mater," said Strange, "was Brush College, more ancient though less pretentious than Harvard, Yale or Princeton. Here I graduated, and I love her memory still. Her academic groves are the boundless forests and prairies of these western wilds: her Pierian springs are the gushing fountains which flow from the rocks and mountain fastnesses. Her Arcadian groves and Orphic songs are the wild woods and the birds of every color and every song, relieved now and then by the base hootings of the night owl, and the weird treble of the whip-poor-will.

"Her curriculum is the philosophy of nature and the mystery of redemption. Her library is the word of God, the discipline and the hymn books, supplemented with trees and brooks and stones, all of which are full of wisdom and sermons and speeches, and her parchments of literary honors are the horse and saddle bags."

Of the forty-one preachers who composed this (1825) conference, there was not a moral or physical coward among them. They had all braved death often, with such variety as to make danger alluring. They had met the spring of the panther, the challenge of the bear and the deadly thrust of the rattlesnake.

FIRST M.E. CHURCH
BUILT IN INDIANA
*Built in 1808
three miles north
of Charleston*

THE RESTORED
BUILDING

THE PROTECTED
STRUCTURE

DEDICATION
SCENE
1925

FIRST METHODIST EPISCOPAL CHURCH
IN INDIANA

Bishop Roberts himself was a lifelong cripple by reason of an encounter with a wild beast during his young manhood. They had all ridden into the teeth of the tornado, swum swollen torrents and gazed into the awful abyss. They had slept in canebrakes and made their bed upon the snow of the prairies, or on the cozy dank soil of the miasmatic swamp. They had wandered hungry and chilled far from a habitation of their fellows to some possible outpost beyond civilization. They knew the grim solitude of the mountains, had been in peril among robbers and ruffians again and again, and had been obliged to meet these ruffians in personal combats at camp-meetings and elsewhere.

They had for the most part preached to the slave in his cabin, and the master in his mansion: in brief they had left the society of friends, the companionship of loved ones, and such comforts as the pioneer enjoyed to seek the worldly, the wicked and the outcast.

By their labors, prayers, tears, sermons and exhortations they builded an empire for God and made the wilderness a safe place for the habitation of man. They perhaps never dreamed of the recompense of reward, such as a grateful posterity pays them today by its acclaim and partiality.

In this 1825 conference was Allen Wiley, who was foremost in founding Asbury, now DePauw University. He was the first secretary of the Indiana Conference and the first agent of the preachers' aid society. With him was James Armstrong—witty, humorous and wise—the first stationed preacher of Indianapolis and the first presiding elder of the Indianapolis District. Here was James Havens, who on entering the ministry could scarcely read or write, yet was destined to become a truly remarkable preacher and administrator and a man of genuine culture.

Havens was blest with Sampson-like physical strength and, like Cartwright, he did not hesitate to level to the ground some son of Anak with his ecclesiastical fist. It was he who whipped the noted Indianapolis bully, Buckhart, and gave him over to the local authorities who jailed him—a humiliation and defeat that wrung from the bruised lips of the preacher-persecutor the doleful lamentation, "Has it come to this that I am whipped by a Methodist preacher?"

Here was Joseph Tarkington, the grandfather of the author, Booth Tarkington, who came to receive his first appointment as a

Methodist preacher after he had taken a five weeks course in the theological clinic of the Indiana wilderness, with James Armstrong, presiding elder.

To this conference came Peter Cartwright from the prairies of Illinois. He was then in the full vigor of his robust manhood, bronzed by exposure, but kingly in aspect, noble in bearing, a stranger to fear, every inch a man. His career was such that, had he been a Jesuit, he would doubtless long since have been canonized and called a Saint Peter the Second!

What more shall I say of Calvin Ruter, Aaron Wood, John Strange, James L. Thompson, George Knight Hester, Steven R. Beggs, George Locke, Eli P. Farmer, Edwin Ray, Charles Holiday, Jesse Walker, and others, who through faith wrought righteousness, stopped the mouths of blasphemers, escaped death, waxed valiant in fight and came out more than conquerors.

Across the century that has come and gone since they wrought for God in this wilderness the Methodist membership and constituency in Indiana has reached 600,000, and this great host up and down country lanes, in villages and populous centers, join with those of us gathered here today and cry, "All hail!" to these heroic pioneer itinerants who for the most part sleep in forgotten graves.

Their wilderness and solitary place has been made to blossom as a rose, and as we surround this ancient Bethel, erected by the Methodist Fathers, let us send up a hallelujah to them across the great divide, assuring them that Methodism is yet strong, virile, vigorous, unchanged in all of its essential aspects and still militant, going forth conquering and to conquer.

Address by Clarence E. Flynn, D.D.

Addresses of felicitation were made by representatives of the four conferences in the Indianapolis Area.

C. E. Flynn, Pastor First Methodist Episcopal Church, Bloomington, Indiana, representing the Indiana Conference, spoke as follows:

We have come here today to live again a vanished hour. By the strange miracle of memory the years drop away and the past is resurrected before us. Quaint but once familiar figures come again and take their places here, and voices long silent speak once more in the stillness of our thoughts.

This place becomes a shrine by virtue of the fact that from it the life of Indiana Methodism has radiated. It was the grain of mustard seed from which grew a widely branching denominational life. The few worshippers who once gathered here were the forerunners of a vast multitude. The local influence which they exerted has become a power which moves in and helps to shape the life of the commonwealth.

We are more numerous than they, but are we better? Has the progress of these decades better taught us the mystic path that leads to the Shining Throne? Does the life of today better testify to the wonder of our common salvation? Are the eyes of the present clearer to see the places where Heaven touches Earth than those that found in this rude altar a Bethel where the gates were opened wide to let the glory of God fall on human hearts?

Even if the elements had been permitted to work their will this old church would not wholly have passed away. Its plain floor and simple seats endure in the broad aisles and polished pews of a thousand others. Its humble walls and crude roof are perpetuated in the pillared arches and massive towers of many successors. The voices that here intoned the hymns of another day are memorialized in every costly organ and modern choir in the temples of the denomination in Indiana. Of it and its life all our work through the years is but a perpetuation.

The clock of God has tolled the year a hundred times since the Illinois Conference met in this place, but the influence of that conference is still in session. The homespun-clad men who sat in that assembly have long since joined the Church Triumphant, but their work lives on. Thought still pictures their hardened hands, their rugged countenances, their simple attire. They were of the indispensable of earth, representatives of the most valuable group of men in the making of the history of any people—the pioneers of the Faith.

They were not princes of the blood, but they were princes by the great rebirth. They were only average men who had given God His way, and in the hands of God no man remains mediocre. They were unusual men because they had accepted an unusual commission. They were enthralled by a great conviction, committed to a great cause, devoted to a great Master, and loyal to a great polity.

They were delivered from the temptation to seek the best places and the largest rewards by the fact that there were none to seek. The hard work and simple fare of a soldier was all they could hope for, and in the success of their efforts they found their chief reward. That conference session was not restless, because there was nothing to be restless about. It was harmonious, because its members had but one purpose—the triumph of the cause. Division does not come where all eyes are single to the glory of God.

The greatest heritage they have left us is not in our majestic temples, our hushed congregations, our pleasant situations. It is in the motive that impelled them, the spirit in which they lived and worked, the way in which they kept faith with God and their brethren. Before their shadowy presence departs may their mantle fall on us anew. May God preserve in us the virtues of our fathers, recreate in us their devotion, and fill us with their passion for conquest and their desire for the triumph of righteousness. Delivered from disloyalty and self-seeking and wholly devoted to the divine purpose, let us press on toward the realization of the dream that thrilled the hearts of departed generations.

Address by Warren W. Wiant, D.D.

W. W. Wiant, Superintendent of the Fort Wayne District of the North Indiana Conference, spoke as follows:

Bishop Leete and brethren of the Indiana Conference:

Methodism of the State of Indiana officially stands today upon hallowed ground. It was in this section of the State and on this very soil almost a century and a quarter ago that the first pioneer preachers of the denomination appeared at the humble cabins of the daring settlers with the good news of the Gospel of Jesus Christ.

The historian tells us that with the cessation of the Indian wars and official land grants by the Government new settlers came into Indiana in large numbers—so many with previous Methodist connections that there were not sufficient preachers to follow and shepherd them. This steady stream of both preachers and people brought into the new country some of the chief essentials in the building of a mighty empire, and the beneficent civilization of this great heart of North America.

They came without any promise or hope of an easy-going, care-free life. New trails had to be blazed in a primeval forest, crude log cabins were erected as shelters from enemy and storm, and with the brawn of hand and mind they exacted from the soil the simple necessities of a livelihood. To those noble men and women of the yesterdays we are eternally indebted. From their souls, like a perennial spring, flowed the undaunted spirit of the pioneer.

In that distant day they faced a rigid, unyielding world of theology, worked out chiefly in cloister and council, which endeavored to present a God, distant and cold, with but little of the human touch and appeal. These prophets of the past came with a new story of the Word of God. What they preached and what they taught had been wrought out in the crucible of human experience. With an undying passion and souls all aglow, they met the people of their day with a heart to heart message of abundant life, and the result was an unparalleled response to the Gospel of Jesus Christ.

They were the men who first dared to lead the way in exposing the degradation and wrongs of human slavery and the evils of the nefarious liquor traffic. Pioneers they were, blazing new spiritual trails over which future generations were to come into possession of the world's highest type of human, religious and civil liberties.

Today we are gathered here to rededicate this little church, so small and humble in materially representing to us the beginnings of our denomination in this great commonwealth as to be almost inconceivable in comparison with the present influence and strength of our numbers. Let us not forget as we tarry here and worship together that our virility and power to cope with the enemies of God and the problems of our day do not rest in wealth and numbers alone. Let us rigidly examine ourselves to see if we have abiding still the "Faith of our Fathers", and have burning on our altars the unconquerable spirit of those heroic men who wrought in the beginning days.

It is my high honor to speak today for the 325 pastors and more than 95,000 laymen of the North Indiana Conference. For this great host of our common family I pledge you undying allegiance to the sterling qualities of mind and soul and to the joyous abandon with which our fathers gave their all to Jesus Christ in those formative days of the Nation and the Church.

May there be likewise in us always a "faith that will not shrink, though pressed by every foe." May our religion and our creeds find their beginnings in those high and holy hours where we meet God at the mercy seat, and live on only as we test them in the ever raging conflicts where unrighteousness and sin and greed prey upon our fellowmen.

Our greatest possessions as Methodists in the world of today are the reckless abandon, the prophetic daring, the never dying zeal and the holy glow with which our fathers first came to this new country. Without these qualities of character and soul we shall have lost our legacy and our right among the peoples of the land.

May we here not only rededicate and reconsecrate this primitive house of worship, but may we rededicate and reconsecrate our souls, our lives, our all to the Master of Men, that in our day we may adequately meet every problem and open up the highways over which may be ever coming the Kingdom of God.

"O master let me walk with thee
In lowly paths of service free;
Tell me thy secret; help me bear
The strain of toil, the fret of care.

"Teach me thy patience, still with Thee
In closer, dearer company,
In work that keeps faith sweet and strong,
In trust that triumphs over wrong."

Address by Reverend Bert D. Beck, D.D.

B. D. Deck, superintendent of the South Bend District of the Northwest Indiana Conference, spoke as follows:

Dear Fathers and Brethren:

It is my privilege and honor to represent the youngest conference in the state. Plans are now under way to celebrate the seventy-fifth anniversary next year. Although twenty years younger than your own conference I am able to bring you the heartiest greetings and assurances of good will from two hundred and fifty-eight preachers and sixty-five thousand laymen.

It would be a great honor to represent this splendid company on any sort of mission anywhere. But it is a matter of keen personal pleasure for me to be their messenger on this happy occasion to this conference where I spent so many happy years and where friendships were formed that shall never die.

From all the Northwest Indiana Conference I bring congratulations to Bishop Leete, J. Ed. Murr and all others who have been active in this movement to preserve this historic church to future generations. What has been done is an achievement worthy of high praise. I was present years ago when J. E. Murr presented the presiding bishop of a session of this conference with a gavel made from the wood taken from this old church. This dream of preserving this church was in his mind then. Numerous times since I have heard him give historical sketches of early Methodism in Indiana. Always the preservation of this old church was at the heart of his appeal. The rest of us were slow to see and appreciate its value. Finally he found an attentive ear and an appreciative heart in Bishop Leete, who has interested both preachers and laymen in the undertaking; hence this successful achievement.

Somehow the West has been slow to value any old things. This is likely due to the fact that nothing is very old here yet. But we stand in danger of letting all of our old things that do have or will have historic value perish before we discover that they will be valuable to future generations. The older section of the country, particularly the New England States, do appreciate their historic centers and are endeavoring to preserve all they can. All of us who have visited that section will bear witness that the old places and things are among the chief interests of those parts. And who can measure the cultural value of them for their own people as well as for the visitors?

It is high time that those of us who make our home in the middle west were awakening to the worth of some of our soon-to-be-old places and things. Lincoln City here in your section of the state is growing in interest each year. Recently I heard three South Bend families who were planning a tourists' route say that their trip would include this shrine. What Lincoln City is as a center of political interest this place will become as a center of religious interest. Just as many of us have journeyed here this day to see this old relic of by-gone days and to participate in the dedication of these new grounds, so in years to come multitudes will make their pilgrimages here to see this the first Methodist church built in Indiana and to carry away with them definite influence for good.

Let us hope that this is just the beginning of a movement that

shall preserve to future generations other like valuable treasures.
We have within the South Bend District Hamilton church which
is reported to be the first Methodist church north of the Wabash
river. It was dedicated by Bishop Simpson. It is used but very
little. It is in need of repair. It ought not be allowed to rot
down. The forward-looking Christ who could see the new age
pictured in the Sermon on the Mount was not blind to the past.
He who taught men to lift up their eyes and look into the future
with faith also said, "This do in rembrance of Me." A keen appreciation of all who have wrought before us is one condition of
our successfully building on the foundation they have laid. To
create in our imaginations the congregation that built this church
and the pastors who served it is to see how we came to our commodious and comfortable churches and to conditions under which
we do church work of which they never dreamed. May there
come upon us today a new and deeper sense of appreciation of
those who laid the foundations of the Church in Indiana, and
please God, more of the Spirit of God who equipped them so well
to do the work of the Church in their day and generation.

Address by President Cameron Harmon, D.D.

President Cameron Harmon, of McKendree College, Lebanon,
Illinois, representing the Southern Illinois Conference, spoke as
follows:

I come to you from Illinois; from her cities' teeming millions;
from her prairies rich with corn; from her rivers gently flowing;
from her churches, schools and homes, to congratulate you men
of God's living own, as hither you come beneath the boughs of
these trees in whose trunks the suns and rains of years are compact, and upon whose leaves God has laid his whispering music,
that you might pass within sacred walls and tread upon holy
ground, filled with God's promise and His miracle.

I felicitate you that through a century you have never permitted the banner of the prince Emanuel to touch the ground, which
was here so boldly and lovingly unfurled to the breezes by hearts
and hands brave and strong. Here came your early fathers with
voices clear, crying in the wilderness, "Make way, for the Lord is
here, strong and mighty for the right." You soldiers of my
Christ caught up the echo, and the chorus has grown for five-score
years, until every hamlet, village and city has heard the glad story

and an innumerable host has followed in His train. In His honor, and to His glory, you have builded homes, schools and churches. Openly you have battled sin, and victory has followed in your train. Out of your ranks valiant soldiers have issued forth to bless mankind, "Wher'er the sun doth his successive journeys run." As truly as Lincoln came this way, drank at your fountains of truth and passed on to breathe blessings upon all mankind, so multitudes of other lights caught a gleam at your altars, and flung their rays far and wide into all the dark corners of the earth, until the story of the Christ brings gladness in every land where sadness yesterday held sway.

Our fathers, who upon these hallowed grounds fought so valiantly for the Master, were not "carried to the skies on flowery beds of ease, while others fought to win the prize and sailed through bloody seas." The friction of life was the keenest possible, but they utilized that very friction the better to prepare themselves for the battles of life. Much depends upon our attitude to the friction of life.

One year ago as wife and I drove through the New England states we came to the point of historic Cape Cod where the Pilgrim fathers first touched American soil. There upon the sand we saw a great vessel which yesterday proudly sailed the seas, but will sail no more forever. We stood by at the ebb-tide, and as the waves of the sea receded, far down upon the smooth sand I saw a bit of glass. I rushed down and secured it and now I hold it in my hand. When first it lodged there the edges were sharp and keen, but now they have disappeared and I can grasp it ever so tightly in my hand and it cuts not the flesh. When first it lodged it was clear, until I could see through it with great ease, but now the friction of the sand has clouded it and its beauty is entirely gone—idly sitting in the sand, permitting the friction of the coming and going of the same to grind it away until it would have entirely disappeared.

One of the first recollections I have of my father was when, as a lad four or five years of age, I carried water to him where he was cutting wheat in the field with a cradle. As I approached him I heard a group of men nearby in conversation, and they declared my father was the best cradler in the community and I was proud of him. I watched as he stooped his athletic back and swung his cradle, cutting the wheat. I followed after him, and by and by he set the cradle upon end, took from his pocket the whetstone and began to hit first one edge and then the other until it almost beat out a tune. The sparks of friction flew thick and fast until by and by he replaced the stone, ran his thumb along the sharpened edge of the scythe, then bending his back once more began to swing the cradle cutting the wheat so smoothly that I fell upon my knees running my hands over the even stubble. The very friction had made keener the blade, and so I find in the battle of life he who walks close to God is but sweetened and strengthened; but the friction of life grows stronger and more effective as the days come and go.

In the battles here fought our forefathers sharpened the blade of truth, went forth into the field white unto the harvest and wrought valiantly for our King, laying the foundations deep and wide upon which we build today. Thanks be unto God for those who have here builded and prayed.

Address by Bishop Leete.

Frederick D. Leete, Resident Bishop of the Indianapolis Area, gave the following address on "Methodism as a Historical Movement":

It is not only the muse of history but the angel of revelation which inspires men to recall the past with ever increasing comprehension and appreciation of its fruitful events. Knowledge and gratitude combine in such expressions as that of the psalmist: "I will remember the works of the Lord; surely I will remember thy wonders of old."

"The dignity of history," to use the fine phrase of Henry Fielding, descends upon those who recall and represent important origins and movements. Methodism gains both in honor and self-respect by the preservation of all facts and monuments which represent God's dealings with this people, and the glorious labors, pains and sacrifices of former days. We are not to worship the past, nor must we bound by its traditions. The dead hand must not be allowed to destroy the power of progress. It should be remembered, however, that civilization and above all Christianity, are outgrowths of life, and must not be cut off from the root which has produced them, or they will wither away.

It may be truly said that no human thought or institution is, strictly speaking, original. The movement known as Methodism had many percursors during the course of religious history. It is said that the Greeks who in early days went to Sicily as colonists believed that the loved river Alphaeus flowed beneath the sea and bubbled up in their new home in the springs of Ortygia. However this may have been, streams do continue beneath the surface of human events and manifest themselves in remote times and distant lands. It may be believed that Methodism is one of the expressions of that entire course of spiritual influence and development which produced the laws, the psalms and the prophecies of Israel and from which came apostolic heroisms, patristic labors, teaching councils, reformatory crusades and all evangelistic and missionary triumphs. It is not too much to say that St. Paul, Chryostom, Augustine, Bernard, Francis of Assisi, Savonarola, Thomas a'Kempis, John Wycliffe, Martin Luther, John Knox, Bunyan, Milton and a host of other pioneers and heralds of Christianity were spiritual brothers of John and Charles Wesley and George Whitefield, and co-founders of the Methodist movement and of its institutions.

Archibald B. D. Alexander in "Thinkers of the Church", speaking of the 19th century says, "Among the forces which helped to elevate the general thought of England at the beginning of the century, the chief place must be given to the Methodist Revival." More specifically he affirms, "Wesley made a new England" and "Wesley created in Britain a new spiritual vision." H. A. Taine, the French critic, in his monumental History of English Literature, while affirming that the early leaders of Methodism triumphed "through austerity and exaggeration which would have ruined them in France," says that the converts of these men "paid their debts, foreswore drunkenness, read the Bible, prayed, and went about exhorting others. Wesley collected them into societies, formed 'classes' for mutual examination and edification, submitted spiritual life to a methodic discipline, built chapels, chose preachers, founded schools, organized enthusiasm." He adds that to this day "the same instinct is still revealed by the same signs; the doctrine of grace survives in uninterrupted energy, and the race, as in the sixteenth century, puts its poetry into the exaltation of the moral sense."

Lecky, the Irish historian and publicist, asserts that "Wesley's sermons were of greater historical importance to England than all the victories by land or sea under Pitt." Matthew Arnold asserts for Wesley "a genius for godliness." Dean Stanley claimed John Wesley as the founder of the Broad Church in the Anglican communion, with which he himself was affiliated. The philosophical F. D. Maurice expresses the conviction that it was Methodism which saved England from being carried into the vortex of the French Revolution.

In 1922 Premier Lloyd George visited City Road Chapel, London, and afterward made an address in behalf of the restoration fund for this venerable house of worship and center of holy memories. In the course of this effort the distinguished Welshman said, "I come from the country that owes more to the Methodist movement of which Wesley was the inspired prophet and leader than to any other movement in its history. Wesley was undoubtedly the greatest religious leader the Anglo-Saxon race ever produced, and the movement of which he was the leader was the greatest religious movement of the past two hundred and fifty years at least. It revived every religious community in the Anglo-Saxon world. It put new blood into the veins of the older communions. Lecky has pointed this out in a very eloquent passage, and so has Sir George Trevelyan in his recent able book. When one bears in mind that all this work was accomplished in connection with the powerful and vigorous race which I prefer to call the Celto-Saxon people, one can imagine its influence has been not merely on the British Empire and America, but on the destiny of the whole world."

Among the many high tributes which have been paid to the Methodist circuit rider in America none has been more adequate and sincere than that of President Theodore Roosevelt. His admiration for virile, effective characters knew no bounds. In the followers of Francis Asbury he recognized men of strong and valiant parts, fit to be heroes and martyrs in the interest of a divine Kingdom and of a redeemed humanity. "Wherever there was a group of log cabins," he says, "there some Methodist circuit rider made his way," and he lauds "nameless and unknown men who perished at the hands of the savages, or by sickness or by flood or storm." It is these "nameless and unknown men" and their successors whom we remember here today, and if the walls could speak the logs of this little first Methodist meeting-house of Indiana would become vocal with the tones of those stalwart souls who once preached or heard the gospel in this small but sacred and symbolic temple, and who came and went through the wilderness on journeys of prodigious danger, toil and love.

Not long since a distinguished United States senator, belonging to another branch of the Church, affirmed that it was the Methodist teaching of universal salvation and free grace which made ours a democratic country. He pointed out the fact that the early colonists were dominated by aristocratic ideals and that their churches taught restrictive and thus aristocratic types of religion. Then came the Methodist itinerants preaching divine love for all men and proclaiming that provision had been made for the redemption and eternal life of every follower of Jesus Christ. This idea, this student of political history said, seized the minds of the people, modified other forms of religion, and rendered impossible types of government which were not based on the common good. Whatever may be thought of this assertion, it must be generally admitted that Methodist influence has always been counted on the side of civil democracy.

It is not now permitted nor is it necessary to trace the modern development of Methodism. One might describe its constant influence upon government, particularly in America, and might name the public men and presidents whom it has produced. The educational institutions which Methodists have founded and maintained in many lands by no means compass the impact of these people upon the intellectual life of the world. Science, literature and art have been enriched by the labors of those whom Methodism has produced and trained. The part taken by its adherents in social reforms has been notable, and has elicited the hostility of the ungodly as well as the praise of the virtuous. Methodist missions have belted the globe, so that the sun never goes down upon their Christian ministries, nor does night ever cause them to cease. Taylor, Thoburn, Butler, Hartzell and other sons of Wesley have gone to the ends of the earth with their wholesome, heart-stirring, life-saving evangel, and they have awakened powers and loosed forces whose efforts will last longer than "the sweet influences of the Pleiades," and will require aeons to compute.

Is it not sufficient for the present to note the brief items which have been stated, and to realize that we are in the midst of a stream of history whose origin and end are wrapped up with divine processes in the web of eternal purpose? Beside this humble log church we stand in deep humility. Who are we, even with our great churches and vast numbers, that we should be the successors of the men of God and the faithful women who planted in the forests and beside the streams the trees of the Lord, now so full of sap, and in whose branches such songs are heard? As we think of McKendree and Roberts, of Lakin, Robertson, Gazaway, Parker, Paine and Hester, and later Cartwright, Strange, Tarkington, the Woods and a host of others, including Ames, Simpson and Bowman, who in the earlier years built upon this foundation, the tiny first church seems to grow in size, and the band of unlettered pioneers and settlers increases into a great host. The basis which was laid more than a century ago for Methodist growth and service in Indiana was broader and stronger than the fathers knew, and seems today to be adequate for all time to come. We are amazed at what God has wrought through the outgrowth of these beginnings. As for ourselves, must we not seek to be worthy of the incidents and personages here recalled? We must and we will go forward with the plan and program of Christian evangelism, civilization and brotherhood "until the day dawn and the day-star arises" to suffuse the hills with the glory of an age in which the will of God shall be done on earth as it is done in Heaven.

Dedication

Bishop Leete, assisted by the Superintendents present, dedicated the new grounds.

Prayer by Reverend Alfred E. Craig, D.D.

Alfred E. Craig, Pastor Trinity Church, Evansville, Indiana, led in prayer as follows:

God of our fathers by whose hand this world was formed, Thee we adore—Christ of our redemption by whose sacrifice men are saved from their sins, Thee we worship—Thou blessed Spirit whose presence is the inspiration of our lives, Thee would we honor in this act of holy dedication.

Our hearts are full of gratitude as we recall Thy manifold mercies. We especially thank Thee for the inheritance which is ours, replete with every measure of blessing. Ours are the rich resources, long preserved in the untouched soil of Thy virgin continent, until the brave pioneer penetrated the wilderness and released this wealth of material blessing. With his strong right arm he felled the forests, drained the swamps, and cleared the waste places where pestilence walked in the darkness and destruction wasted at noon-day. He labored, and we enjoy the abundant fruits of his toil.

But we have met today to recall especially the services of those brave adventurers of faith who counted not their lives dear unto them if they might thereby fulfill their Lord's commission to carry the inspiration and hope of the gospel to those lonely settlers, sparsely scattered throughout the wilderness waste. To achieve this brave enterprise they penetrated forests, forded streams, encountered wild beasts and still wilder men, suffering all the privations of the early settler's poverty as good soldiers of Jesus Christ. Thus they laid the foundation of our beloved Methodism as they preached the glorious gospel of Christ's salvation wherever men and women might assemble, in cabins, in barns, in leafy groves, in humble meeting houses erected out of the logs of the primitive forest, hewn with their own strong right hands. In thy good providence one of these humble meeting houses has been preserved and we, the proud sons of these noble fathers, here rededicate it, to stand as an altar where generations to come may light the torches of their zeal and kindle the flame of their inspiration to continue in their day the same blessed ministry the fathers gave to their generation.

May this day's enterprise be crowned with thy divine approval, and to Thee will be all the honor and glory. Amen.

Memorial Conference Session.

The Conference visited the old Illinois Conference building where the Illinois Conference session of 1825 was held.

The Conference was convened for a short session by Bishop Leete.

The Secretary read the roll of the members of the session of 1825.

W. S. Bovard, D.D., president of the Board of Education of the Methodist Episcopal Church, gave an address on "Present Day Methodism."

Bishop Robert Roberts' hymnal, owned by Mrs. Iron of Crawfordsville; James Garner's hymnal, now owned by J. E. Murr of New Albany; James Garner's discipline of 1813, now owned by Judge Poindexter of Jeffersonville, and the Bible owned by Rev. James Garner, now in the keeping of Mrs. E. E. Long of Jeffersonville were exhibited to the large company present.

On motion the Conference adjourned. The benediction was pronounced by E. R. Zaring, D.D., pastor of the First Methodist Episcopal Church, Columbus, Indiana.

GREENCASTLE
INDIANA
CHURCH

NORTH
CHURCH
INDPLS.

HIGH
STREET
CHURCH
MUNCIE

PROJECTED ENTERPRISES

Facing the Future

•••••••••••••

NEW PROJECTS.

By Claude H. King, D.D.

EXPANDING programs, increasing memberships, fuller realization of responsibilities and growing needs of constituencies are demanding more adequate buildings and equipment. The new church building projects already under way or assured are of a type that reflects the thoughtful purpose and determination of Methodism in this area to enter more largely into the character-building movements demanded by new and changed conditions. These programs vary from single units for educational, social, or recreational work to complete new auditorium and Sunday school facilities.

Some of those which give the fullest promise of immediate realization are as follows:

North Church, Indianapolis, has on hand assets in property, pledges and material, amounting to two hundred and eighty thousand dollars toward its six hundred and fifty thousand dollar program. When completed, this church will have an auditorium sixty-one feet by one hundred and two feet, and an educational unit prepared to care for the religious education demands of membership and constituency.

Greencastle church has its plans and specifications completed. This project will cost approximately three hundred thousand dollars and is designed to meet the needs of a university center.

LaPorte church has a two hundred and fifty thousand dollar building that is almost completed. It will have the equipment of a strictly modern church.. This church will be ready for dedication sometime during the summer of 1928.

High Street Church, Muncie, is engaged in a project which, including real estate, will cost more than four hundred thousand dollars. This building will be a modernized Gothic type of architecture, providing an auditorium with a seating capacity of thirteen hundred, and a complete and modern church school unit, providing class rooms and equipment for a school of fifteen hundred.

River Park Church, South Bend, already has the basement walls of a seventy thousand dollar addition to its present plant. This unit will provide adequate physical equipment for the membership and constituency. The same may be said of the West Michigan Church, Indianapolis.

Indiana Harbor Church is assured of a three-story educational wing addition which will provide gymnasium and class rooms.

New Carlisle church is beginning extensive remodeling of its old building, with a complete new basement and a new educational unit.

The Methodist Temple, Terre Haute, formerly First and Centenary churches, has plans for a three hundred thousand dollar plant, but has not yet actually begun operation.

Central Church, Richmond, the merged First and Grace congregations, has completed its present financial program with a subscription of two hundred thousand dollars besides its present properties, and the beginning of construction is set at an early date.

OPEN DOORS OF OPPORTUNITY

By Manfred C. Wright, S.T.B.

The Indianapolis Area presents ideal ground for four or five major types of church activity now rising to commanding importance.

There is the rural field. In agriculture Indiana has few superiors, while southern Illinois holds the center of the corn belt. Here, then, is offered the finest field for rural church work. Hewitt's "Steeples Among the Hills"—that classic in rural New England church achievement—might have been written on Hoosier soil as voicing our country problems and needs. The demand for well trained and specialized pastoral service, with lengthened pastoral appointment, covering sufficient years to master and develop a given field, holds here as much as anywhere. Opportunities for monumental service loom here just as large as they do in Plainfield, Vermont. In rural Indiana and southern Illinois the consolidation of public schools has brought to the countryside the best educational talent and methods. Similar demands call for skillful development of country church work. Another quadrennium should register for the Indianapolis Area extended progress in the rural field.

No less inviting is the industrial field. In industry Indiana also ranks among the first states of the Union. Vast coal fields hold an army of miners. In railroading, numerous trunk lines cross these states east and west, and north and south; while in aviation flying lanes are multiplying across this territory. Every good sized town has become a manufacturing center; while the Calumet region, as a second Pittsburg, is the modern wonder of the industrial world.

In such a vast industrial area a companion book to "Steeples Among the Hills" might be written under the title, "Spires Among Smokestacks," to sound the depths of industrial church work needs. And none the less would there appear a like demand for a specially trained ministry fitted for the enlarging task.

Industrial expansion bulges the growth of cities; and along with increasing sky-scrapers runs the demand for skillful sky-pilots. Increasing industrial efficiency demands improvement in church methods; while, ramifying the industrialism and commercialism of this age, must be applied the saving principles of the Gospel of Christ.

Not for a quadrennium only but for a half century to come the ground as occupied by the Indianapolis Area will witness strategic battles for Christian progress in the field of industry; while vast armies of workmen and their families in this strategic center will call for divinely passionate shepherds no less than do verdant hills and quiet villages—they will also call for church programs adapted to new, and changeful, and intensive conditions. May the church we love not fail in this major opportunity! May the Indianapolis Area answer this heroic challenge!

Related to the industrial field is that of immigrant populations. Originally Indiana drew finest racial streams from eastern states and from southern neighboring sections. Today later immigrant streams conglomerate in Hammond, Whiting, East Chicago and Gary. The Calumet Region holds immigrant populations as varied and as interesting as may be found anywhere in the United States. Other centers, as South Bend and Mishawaka, have similar masses scarcely less numerous.

What a field here offers as that of sheep not having a shepherd! The challenge has been met in part by the Board of Home Missions and Church Extension. A newly erected monumental pile in Lake Michigan's "Steel City" marks our outstanding attempt in architecture to match program with cosmopolitan life. Working plants built by the Woman's Home Missionary Society in Fort Wayne and Gary, in varied adaptation to striking needs, mark the way of immigrant feet to a finer Christian Americanism.

But as yet the immigrant wilderness has been but scarcely entered. A wider shepherding must be done, to bring the wanderers from far lands into the fold. Investments of life, of money, of educated talent in settlement work must go forward. Valuable leaders as well as redeemed populations will come from this effort. When the writer of this article was a pastor in Whiting twenty years ago, Oscar Ahlgren, then a lad from Finland, found a spiritual home in our Whiting church. Last winter that boy, grown to manhood, with collegiate training, was the chairman of the educational committee of Indiana's highest law-making body. Other such possible leaders await development as the fruitage of the Indianapolis Area. Shall we not enter more widely this open door? No finer work offers than the culture of the immigrant mind and heart in American character and Christian purpose.

Related to each of the foregoing lies the field of week-day religious education. Hitherto the weakness of the Protestant method has been in the attempt to crowd our whole religious education program into the Sabbath day. The result of this attempt has been to weaken our public worship and to fail of largest success in all of our subsidiary objectives. Now the way appears to relieve this congestion by putting much of our religious training in the midst of the week.

Four plans for such instruction appear. The mid-week church night offers fine instructional opportunity for intensive training for one or two seasons of the year. On these evenings the whole church in groups assemble for standard courses in training classes. The daily Vacation Bible School provides three or four or five weeks of intensive training for children, either managed as a local church school or as a community affair. Week-day religious education in regular daily classes throughout the public school year, under separate church management or in cooperation with other churches and with the public schools, grows with commanding importance. Any and all of these plans gradually projected should find feasible room in all the churches of the Indianapolis Area.

Before the young people of the Area stands the widening door of the summer and mid-winter institutes. Indiana Epworth Leagues pioneered this field. Now the field widens alluringly. Our present institute buildings can not hold the annually enlarging throngs. Missionary societies also are opening this door wider to young people for intensive training. The institute plan has come to occupy largely the ground long held by the camp meeting. To occupy the ground more fully new sites for institutes call for development which in the years ahead may provide special training for every young Methodist in the Area.

Today, as before a former pioneering generation, these widening fields open their doors of opportunity. May the progress registered during the past two quadrenniums of the Indianapolis Area urge us on to wider, as well as to more intensive, tasks. Entering these doors do we make progress as effective and far-visioned Methodists.

TOMORROW

By William Grant Seaman, Ph.D., D.D.

Tomorrow is promising in the Indianapolis Area. The leadership of the Area has given full recognition to the fact that there are laws of spiritual wellbeing, and that what tomorrow will be is determined by the forces set in motion today.

No policy could be more far-seeing than that which has been promoted in this Area, of having Christ recognized in every home, for the home more than any other institution can enthrone

Christ in the heart. In no way can Christ's dominance of the future be made more certain.

Within the bounds of the Indianapolis Area there has been great interest in religious education. In this Area was begun the recent move for religious education for public school children. Some twelve to fifteen thousand children are now receiving instruction in these classes. This Area shares in the new interest in the work of the Sunday school and is profiting by thought given to the courses for study, emphasis upon efficiency in instruction, and activities planned for organized classes. This Area has four of the best of the summer institutes, which help greatly to promote the work of the Sunday schools, and which are putting new life into work with young people, both in the Sunday schools and the Leagues. All this will bear fruit tomorrow in extending the sway of Christ over more lives, in an enrichment of the spiritual life, in a more intelligent membership and in a more devoted and skillful leadership.

There is great promise also in the work of the institutions of higher education. The church in this Area is quite well supplied with colleges. Increases in endowment, improvements in buildings, enlargement of teaching staff and additions to equipment have prepared these for more efficient work. There has been also a notable development of "foundations" at state institutions of higher learning. There are signs that in all these institutions a new attention is being given to the life of the students as well as to their instruction. Through these institutions increasing numbers of our young people will be tied to the church and will share in the fuller life Christ came to bring.

The leadership of the Area has given careful attention to the choice of strategic locations for churches and to the construction of more beautiful and better adapted buildings. Along with this there has been a broadening of the service rendered by the churches. Thus the church faces tomorrow with her forces better aligned and equipped to meet the challenge that confronts her.

This Area has been the scene of some of America's most sweeping revival movements. There still are victories in such efforts, and while the urbanization of society has thrown the church into something of confusion as to its evangelistic methods, there are renewed signs of an evangelistic passion and of a set purpose to find a way to bring "the power of God unto salvation" to bear upon a needy world.

But the great promise of tomorrow lies in the fact that still "mankind is incurably religious" and that the pursuing love of the Father, the atoning sacrifice of a crucified Christ and the wooing of the Spirit are persistently at work for and in the hearts of men.

Methodist Episcopal Facts

....

GLEANED FROM METHODIST YEAR BOOK FOR 1928

THE Methodist Episcopal Church has 25,358 Sunday schools with an enrollment of 4,183,985. About 200,000 members are added to the church each year from these schools. They give about a million and a half dollars yearly to World Service.

It has 19,332 traveling preachers; 1,649 members on trial in the various conferences; and 15,261 local preachers. It has church and parsonage property with an estimated valuation of $479,172,-746. It paid for various items of local expense in 1927, $78,374,-990, and during the quadrennium $305,898,911. It gave to World Service in 1927 $8,330,352, and for the quadrennium around $34,000,000.

The Methodist Episcopal Church in the United States has a record for 1927 of 198,194 baptisms, 168,511 preparatory members received, and of 4,296,100 full members on the roll. During the quadrennium 854,115 baptisms were administered, and 760,700 preparatory members were received.

It has twenty-five ministers over ninety years of age. Of these one, J. B. Lathrop of Greensburg, Indiana, is 102, and another, Edward S. Best of Malden, Massachusetts, is 103. It has four pastors who have served in their present pastorates for a period of twenty years, two who have served twenty-one years, one who has served twenty-two years, two who have served twenty-three years, one who has served twenty-seven years, one who has served thirty-one years, three who have served thirty-two years, and one who has served thirty-three years.

The General Conference of 1928 will be the thirty-fifth general conference. The first was held at Baltimore in 1792. At that time each preacher in full connection was a member. Later that conference became a delegated body. In 1800 six annual conferences were represented. In 1928 one hundred thirty-seven annual conferences will be represented.

The church has elected in all ninety-eight bishops. Of these forty-two are still living and thirty-seven are effective. Five are retired and fifty-six deceased. Fifteen missionary bishops have been elected. Of these four were later elected general superintendents. Two are retired and nine are deceased.

The Methodist Episcopal Church is responsible for the following educational institutions in the United States: forty-three colleges and universities, two junior colleges, five graduate schools, seven schools of commerce, three schools of dentistry, four schools of engineering, eight law schools, three medical schools, ten schools of theology, one school of pharmacy, one school of forestry, one school of education, one school of religious education, and twenty-eight secondary schools.

At the present time we have sixty-seven Wesley Foundations. They employ forty-two full time workers, many part time workers, and eight inter-denominational workers. One hundred thousand Methodist students are now enrolled in tax supported schools. The church contributed about 75,000 in 1927 to be distributed for work in fifty-one centers.

We have in America seventy-nine hospitals, forty-five homes for the aged, forty-six childrens' homes, forty-nine deaconess homes with two branch homes and eight stations, twenty-three homes for business girls, and ten schools for deaconess training. There are sixty-three centers of deaconess work in Europe.

In America the Methodist Episcopal Church publishes one bi-monthly review, ten weeklies in English, and one weekly in German. In addition to these ten semi-official and unofficial periodicals are published in behalf of its work. In foreign fields it publishes or participates in the publication of periodicals as follows: Africa, two; Central America and Panama, one; China, eight; India, twenty-two; Japan, one; Korea, three; Malaysia and Netherlands Indies, two; Mexico, two; Philippine Islands, four; South America, eight; Austria, Hungary, and Jugo Slavia, seven; Baltic States, five; Bulgaria, one; Denmark, one; Finland, three; Germany, ten; Italy, three; Norway, three; Scandinavia, one; Sweden, four; Switzerland, four.

The benevolent activities of the Methodist Episcopal Church are carried on through the following authorized agencies: The Board of Foreign Missions; The Board of Home Missions and

Church Extension; The Board of Education; The Board of Pensions and Relief; The Board of Temperance, Prohibition, and Public Morals; The Board of Hospitals, Homes, and Deaconess Work; The Woman's Foreign Missionary Society; and The Woman's Home Missionary Society. It participates in the work of the American Bible Society. The Board of Education comprises the Departments of Educational Institutions, the Epworth League, Educational Institutions for Negroes, and Church Schools. The official benevolent agencies of the church are unified under the World Service Commission.

The Methodist Book Concern was established in 1789 with a borrowed capital of $600. December 1, 1926 its assets were $8,111,964.28. Down to December 31, 1926 it had distributed to retired ministers, their widows and orphans $7,454,908. It employs more than 1,100 people with an annual pay roll of more than $1,100,000. It distributes more than a billion pages of Sunday school literature each year. It bound more than 2,400,000 books during the year 1926.

Constitutions

....

CONSTITUTION OF INDIANAPOLIS AREA

Preamble

IN ORDER to carry out the purposes of the General Conference of the Methodist Episcopal Church in the establishment of the Indianapolis Area, and to so relate together the conferences of the area that their work may be united in spirit and co-ordinated in activity, a meeting held at Central Avenue Methodist Episcopal Church, Indianapolis, July 15, 1920, and which was attended by representatives of all the districts in the state, and by all the district superintendents, adopted for the approval of the annual and lay conferences the provisions of this instrument. The declared purpose is to further all the undertakings of Methodism, its evangelical program, its church building and development, its social service, especially the work of its educational and philanthropic institutions, and its efforts in conjunction with other public bodies to assure the civic and moral welfare of the peoples and communities of the state. The Area and State Councils established by this constitution shall have power to prosecute the work of Methodism within their jurisdiction in harmony with the general policy of the Methodist Episcopal Church and the vested rights of the annual conferences.

CONSTITUTION

ARTICLE I: *Councils.*

There shall be an Area Council, a State Council, Conference Councils, District Councils (if desired), and City Councils (if desired by the Bishop or district superintendent.)

ARTICLE II: *Area Council.*

The Area Council shall be composed of the members of the conference councils of the area, namely, the Indiana, the North Indiana, the Northwest Indiana, and the Southern Illinois Conferences. The resident bishop, one head of each chain of institu-

173

tions and the head of each independent institution officially recognized by the area, as well as one officer of each conference Epworth League institute, designated by that body, the area secretary, and the editor of the official paper shall be members of the Area Council without election. The officers shall consist of the resident bishop, who shall preside when present: a vice-president for each of the conferences of the area, the secretary and treasurer of the State Council, and of such other officers as the work of the Council may require. The conference presidents shall be vice-presidents of the Area Council, and in the absence of the resident bishop shall designate one of their number to preside. The committees of the Area Council shall consist of the committees of the State Council, together with proportional representation from the Southern Illinois Conference. The Area Council shall have such powers as are implicit in the creation of the area by the General Conference.

Article III: *Indiana State Council*

This instrument was adopted by all the conferences of the State.

1. Organization. The State Council shall be composed of the members of the conference councils elected by the conferences which are contained within the state of Indiana, fifteen pastors and fifteen laymen, elected at large annually by the State Council, on nomination of the Executive Committee together with the resident bishop, the area secretary, the official editor, one officer of each conference Epworth League institute, designated by that body, and one head of each chain of institutions and the head of each independent institution officially recognized by the State Council. The officers shall consist of the resident bishop, who shall preside when present; a vice-president for each of the conferences of the state; the secretary and treasurer, and of such other officers as the work of the Council may require. The conference presidents shall be vice-presidents of the State Council, and in the absence of the resident bishop shall designate one of their number to preside.

2. Expense Fund. The expense of the work of the State Council shall be met by an apportionment on this basis: Charges paying less than $1,000 including house rent shall be asked to contrib-

ute $1.00 per annum. Charges paying $1,000 to $1,499 including house rent shall be asked to contribute $2.00 per annum. Charges paying $1,500 to $1,999 including house rent shall be asked to contribute $6.00 per annum. Charges paying $2,000 or more per annum including house rent shall be requested to contribute $9.00. Charges paying $3,000 or more including house rent per annum shall be asked to pay $12.00. Charges paying $4,000 or more including house rent shall be asked to contribute $15.00.

3. Committees. The following shall be the standing committees, the resident bishop and the area secretary to be members ex-officio of all committees of the State Council:

(1) An Executive Committee, composed of the resident bishop, the official editor, all district superintendents, and one pastor and layman from each district of the conferences within the state, to be elected by the members of the Council who represent the district. This committee shall, as part of its duties, prepare and publish an area inventory and prospectus. To it shall also be referred and it shall have charge of topics referring to the development and correlation of institutions, the need of any area building projects, or other co-operative movements, including the promotion of Disciplinary benevolent campaigns and the distribution of church literature.

(2) Public and Personal Evangelism.

(3) Methodist Institutions - Colleges, Homes, Area Headquarters, etc.

(4) World Service at Home and Abroad. Educational and Financial Campaigns.

(5) Christian Literature.

(6) Government and Legislation - Proposed Statutes, Law Enforcement.

(7) Charities and Reforms.

(8) Social and Economic Conditions - Agricultural, Commercial, Industrial.

(9) Public Education.

(10) Sunday Schools and Young People's Work. Training Conferences, Institutes, Boy and Girl Scouts, etc. County Organizations.

(11) Life Service.

(12) Ministerial Supply and Training.

(13) Area Men's Committee - Finance, Lay Leadership, Lay Conferences.

(14) Area Women's Committee.

(15) Conference and District Programs, Chautauquas, County Rallies.

(16) Publicity.

The Women's and Men's Area Committees shall become as large as they shall see fit to make them, and the remaining committees shall, with the exception of the Executive Committee above, be composed of six members, two from each conference, with as few duplications as possible. A committee of two from each conference, with the bishop, shall be authorized to assign Council members to the standing committees and report the same to the secretary for publication.

4. Incorporation. The officers of the State Council are empowered to take the legal steps necessary for incorporation of the State Council.

5. Meetings. The State Council shall meet annually, or at such times as shall be called by the president or by the request of two-thirds of the district superintendents of the state.

ARTICLE IV: Conference Councils.

Conference councils of the Indianapolis Area shall be composed of delegates elected annually by each district conference, to represent the districts on the basis of one minister and one layman for each four thousand full members of the churches and for three-fourths excess fraction of four thousand found in the district. Each district superintendent shall be one of the ministerial delegates of the district without election. In addition there shall be selected one pastor and one layman from each district as reserves. The conference councils shall have authority to fill vacancies within their own numbers. All general officers of the area and each head of a chain of institutions or separate institutions recognized by the state or conference shall be a member of the conference council without election. The conference council shall elect its own president, who shall occupy the chair when

Superintendents *of* Indianapolis Area Districts

Southern Illinois

CHARLES B. WHITESIDE, FRANK O. WILSON

WALTER M. BROWN   CHARLES L. PETERSON   WALTER H. WHITLOCK

North Indiana

WARREN W. WIANT   F. F. THORNBURG   WILLIAM T. ARNOLD

LAYTON C. BENTLEY   U. S. A. BRIDGE   CHARLES H. SMITH

present, unless the resident bishop presides. It shall also elect such other officers and committees as may be desired.

Article V: *District Councils*

District councils may be elected by the districts for their own work, if the district superintendent desires. They may have such officers and committees as seem best locally.

Article VI: *City Councils.*

City councils, formal or informal in organization, to act separately or with local Methodist unions, may be instituted wherever they are desired and assembled by the resident bishop or by the district superintendents.

By-Laws

(1) The annual meeting of the Area and State Councils shall be held after the fall conferences of the area, at a date announced by the bishop after the dates of the fall conferences are fixed.

(2) Amendments to this constitution may be proposed by a majority vote of an annual conference or in the Area or State Council by any member or members. It shall become effective when adopted by a two-thirds vote of the Area or State Council at its annual meeting.

(3) Members of the Council shall retain office till their successors are chosen.

(4) The institutions to which mention is made in the constitution include DePauw University, Evansville College, Indiana and Purdue Wesley Foundations, Methodist hospitals, and such other institutions as shall from time to time receive the official recognition of the Council.

(The following have been added by subsequent actions: Conference Corresponding Secretary of W.F.M.S. Conference President, W.H.M.S. President, Conference Laymen's Association; Conference Secretary Preachers' Aid Society.)

CONSTITUTION OF CITY COUNCIL

ARTICLE I.
Title.

This society shall be called the City Council and Church Extension Society of Indianapolis, Indiana.

ARTICLE II.
Membership.

All annual contributors to the funds of the City Council, together with the Board of Managers, shall be members of the Council.

ARTICLE III.
Officers.

The superintendent of the Indianapolis District shall be the president of the City Council. The other officers shall be three vice-presidents, an executive secretary (in case one is employed), a recording secretary, and a treasurer; all of whom shall be elected by the Council at its annual meeting on nomination of the Executive Committee of the Council. The resident bishop shall be ex officio honorary president of the City Council.

ARTICLE IV.
Board of Managers.

Sec. 1. The Board of Managers shall consist of the officers of the Council, the pastors of the city churches, a lay delegate from each church to be elected annually by the official board on nomination of the pastor, and not to exceed twenty members at large to be nominated by the Executive Committee. Honorary members may be elected on nomination of the Executive Committee.

Sec. 2. Regular meetings of the Board of Managers shall be held semi-annually in the months of October and April, at such time and place as the By-Laws shall determine. Special meetings may be called by the president or recording secretary on request of the Executive Committee. The Board of Managers shall adopt By-Laws which do not conflict with this Constitution, fill vacancies in their own number or among the officers, act on appropriations to be made, establish the general policy of the Council, and adopt measures judged to be expedient for the promotion of its interests.

Sec. 3. At the regular meeting in October officers shall be elected and the accounts of the treasurer shall be audited.

Sec. 4. Fifteen members shall constitute a quorum of the Board of Managers.

ARTICLE V.

Duties of Officers.

The officers shall perform the usual duties which pertain to the officers of the Council.

ARTICLE VI.

Trustees.

The duties of the trustees are defined in the acts of incorporation of the Council.

Sec. 1. There shall be a board of nine trustees. The president, the resident bishop, and the treasurer of the Council shall be three. The remainder are to be elected at the annual meeting of the Board of Managers in classes of two, each class to serve for three years.

Sec. 2. All real property owned by the Council shall be managed by the Board of Trustees under the direction of the Executive Committee of the Board of Managers. The trustees shall turn over the income of any property held for the uses of the Council as directed. The Board of Trustees shall not authorize the sale, transfer or mortgage of any real property of the Council nor the alienation of the proceeds of such property without the approval of the Executive Committee.

ARTICLE VII.

Executive Committee.

The Executive Committee shall consist of the officers, six pastors, and fourteen laymen to be elected annually by the Board of Managers.

Article VIII.

Annual Meeting.

The fiscal year of the Council shall begin October 1. At the annual meeting the following order of business shall be observed:

1. Devotions.
2. Minutes of previous meeting.
3. Report of president or executive secretary.
4. Report of treasurer.
5. Report of executive committee.
6. Addresses.
7. Election of officers.
8. Miscellaneous.
9. Adjournment.

Article IX.

Amendments.

This Constitution may be altered or amended by a two-thirds vote of the members present at any regular meeting of the Board of Managers, providing that notice of the proposed change has been given at the previous meeting, or at least two months previously to the Executive Committee.

Personnel

••••••••••••

PASTORAL APPOINTMENTS 1927-1928

••••••••••••

INDIANA CONFERENCE

Corrected to date by H. W. Baldridge, Secretary

Bloomington District

E. H. Boldrey, D.S., Bloomington, Ind.

Arlington..................(E. M. Davis)
Asbury and Ashboro..........J. F. Dyer
    R. R., Worthington, Ind.
Bedford—
    Circuit..................A. W. Jarboe
    First Church..............J. N. Greene
Bloomfield..................F. T. Taylor
Bloomington—
    Fairview................E. F. Schneider
    First Church..............C. E. Flynn
Bowling Green..........(C. J. Galbraith)
Brooklyn....................R. J. Crider
Center Point............(Theodore Eisert)
Clay City..................C. E. Adams
Cloverdale..................J. W. Harmon
Cory........................A. L. Beatty
Ellettsville................R. C. Minton
Freedom....................V. V. Stauffer
Gosport ....(John Ragle)
Harrodsburg................D. W. Noble
Heltonville................J. O. Cresap
Jasonville..................M. E. Abel
Linton......................O. E. Haley
Lyons......................W. H. McGowan

Martinsville—
    Circuit..................(C. S. Bair)
    First Church..........G. V. Hartman
Mitchell..................H. H. Allen
Mooresville..................B. B. Shake
Morgantown..................C. R. Fitz
Nashville.........Kenneth Vandeventer
Newberry..............(Robert Walker)
Owensburg..............(Paul Haywood)
    Mineral, Ind.
Patricksburg and
    Vandalia..................J. J. Gettinger
Quincy..................... Roma Fields
    718 E. Seminary St., Greencastle
Rivervale..................E. A. Hartsaw
Shiloh and Mill Grove (Oscar Kaylor)
    Spencer, Ind., R.F.D.
Simpson..................(W. J. Ellis)
    Solsberry, Ind.
Solsberry.................. (Virgil Pate)
    Stanford, Ind.
Spencer....................N. G. Talbott
Switz City..................R. M. Taylor
Waverly..................(Fred Reynolds)
Worthington..............J. A. Sumwalt

Connersville District

J. T. Scull, D.S., Rushville, Ind.

Arlington................(W. R. Teltoe)
Bath................(B. M. DeCroes)
Boston................Shields White
Brookville................G. A. Smith
Brownsville................A. E. Chastain
Carthage................Lee Jarrett
Clarksburg................J. W. Trowbridge
Clifty................Merritt Machlan
College Corner................W. S. Rader
Connersville—
  First Church................J. S. Ward
  Grand Avenue................P. S. May
  Main Street................J. R. Flanigan
Everton................W. L. Mitchell
Fairfield................(G. C. Housman)
  R.F.D. 2, Brookville, Ind.
Fairland................(William Ryland)
Flat Rock................M. E. Baker
Glenwood................W. A. Hartsaw
Greensburg................C. W. Whitman
Laurel................(R. A. Grismore)

Liberty................C. M. Reed
Manilla................G. J. Pickett
Metamora................(T. H. Robinson)
Milroy................H. O. Kisner
Milton................Wilbur C. Watkins
Morristown................Homer Manuel
Mt. Carmel................(G. H. Edwards)
  R.F.D. 4, Brookville, Ind.
New Palestine................R. O. LaHue
Rushville................E. L. Hutchins
St. Paul................E. A. Gillum
Sandusky................(I. T. Rogers)
  R.F.D. Greensburg, Ind.
Shelbyville—
  First Church................L. T. Freeland
  Trinity................(J. B. Campbell)
  West Street................R. R. Cross
Waldron................R. O. Pearson
Westport................H. G. Ramsey
Winchester................(Golden Northern)
  Shelbyville, Ind.

Evansville District

George H. Murphy, D.S., Evansville, Ind.

Birdseye................(Meyers McKinney)
Blue Grass................C. A. Shake
  R.R., Evansville, Ind.
Boonville................Elmer St. Clair
Cannelton................W. R. Ashby
Chandler................A. R. Does
Chrisney................(Raymond Skelton)
Cynthiana................(R. J. Stephens)
Dale................(E. M. Dunbar)
Epworth................(L. D. Sander)
  2703 Mulberry St., Evansville
Evansville—
  Asbury................E. A. Boston
  Bayard Park................J. M. Walker
  Central................W. W. Bollinger
  Howell................T. E. Adams
  Old North................W. F. Walters
  St. James................Amos Boren
  Simpson................C. P. McKinney

  Trinity................A. E. Craig
  Wesley................M. O. Robbins
Fort Branch................E. F. Shake
Francisco................(L. R. Morlen)
Gentryville................(D. H. Rosier)
Grand View................(A. P. Bentley)
Hatfield................(S. E. Stroud)
Hazelton................(W. A. Skelton)
Huntingburg................E. H. Omohundro
Lynnville................(J. A. Cottrell)
Millersburg................(M. L. Tullis)
  Chandler, R.R. 1
Mt. Vernon................R. E. Badger
Mt. Vernon—
  Lower Circuit................(O. C. Haas)
Mt. Vernon—
  Upper Circuit................(Albert Hedges)
Newburg................(H. J. Kieser)
New Harmony................E. A. Robertson
Newtonville................(J. C. Cissna)

Oakland City................H. A. Sprague
Oriole..........................(Albert Harris)
Owensville........................ Oscar Jean
Patoka..............................D. M. Boyd
Poseyville...................... A. S. Bastin
Princeton—
    First Church................R. L. Phillips
    Memorial......................W. F. Fink
Rockport........................Frank Lenig

Rockport Circuit......(James McCord)
Rome............................(R. D. Biven)
Selvin..............................Claud Oskins
Tell City............................J. I. Meyer
Troy..................................A. Brinklow
Union and Oak Grove,
                  (William Warner)
Yankeetown....................A. E. Morris
           Newburg, Ind., R.R.

Indianapolis District

Orien W. Fifer, D.S., Indianapolis, Ind.

Acton...................(Norris Wolfgang)
Beech Grove.....................J. D. Jeffery
Belleville.................... (R. H. Myers)
    422 Anderson St., Greencastle, Ind.
Castleton...........................E. E. Jones
Cumberland and Old
    Bethel............................E. P. Jewett
Edgewood.................... H. M. Pattison
Edinburg............................C. H. Rose
Franklin......................R. A. Ragsdale
Friendswood and Bethel (John Yakel)
Glenns Valley.............. James Harrell
Greenwood.............H. C. Clippinger
Henninger....................(S. L. Welker)
Indianapolis—
    Arlington......(George E. Andrews)
    Barth Place...................T. J. Hart
    Bellaire.......................W. B. Grimes
    Blaine Ave..................A. L. Bennett
    Brightwood.................V. B. Hargitt
    Broad Ripple...............M. A. Farr
    Broadway..............John W. McFall
    Capitol Avenue.............J. G. Moore
    Central Avenue.........F. L. Roberts
    East Park................A. J. Spaulding
    East Tenth.....George S. Henninger
    East 29th..................Maurice Kerr
    Edwin Ray...................W. T. Jones
    Fifty-first......................J. F. Seelig

Fletcher Place..............W. F. Russell
Forest Manor..........(R. F. Laycock)
Fountain Street...........R. R. Kelley
Garfield Ave...................C. S. Black
Hall Place...............M. H. Reynolds
Heath Memorial...........L. G. Carnes
Irvington..............J. B. Rosemurgy
Madison Ave...........(Paul Hargitt)
Meridian Street........Virgil E. Rorer
Merritt Place...........................
Morris Street........ C. L. Griffith
North Church...............C. P. Gibbs
Roberts Park....Edwin W. Dunlavy
Shelby St................J. W. J. Collins
School St................(R. F. Laycock)
Trinity....................... Vern Krause
West Michigan..............C. M. Kroft
West Washington.....L. H. Kendall
Woodside.................W. G. Morgan
Lawrence....................T. G. Godwin
Maywood..............John H. Hanger
Mt. Auburn and
    Glade ....(Arthur Palmer)
Nineveh..............(C. V. McMillan)
Southport and
    East 29th ....F. W. Davis
Trafalgar................(George Curtis)
West Newton........ H. A. Broadwell
Whiteland.................. J. R. Bolin

New Albany District

J. S. Murr, D.S., New Albany, Ind.

Austin..........................V. M. Suddarth
Blocher.................(Russell Huffman)
Campbellsburg........(N. M. Rumbley)
Canton...........................(E. L. Bates)
R.R. 2, Salem, Ind.
Central Barren...........H. J. Propheter
R.R., New Salisbury, Ind.
Charlestown................H. C. Newman
Corydon ....C. F. Glick
DePauw......................(G. S. Sutton)
Elizabeth ....(H. G. Wedding)
Embury Ct................(E. G. Arnold)
2405 Shelby St., New Albany.
Fredericksburg...........(C. O. Carnes)
French Lick....................C. O. Morin
French Lick Ct.....(C. E. Waggoner)
Georgetown............ (Horace Sonner)
Greenville......................(J. C. Gray)
Henryville................. Charles Holmes
Jeffersonville—
Maple Street................E. A. Clegg
Park Place............E. C. McKinney
Wall Street...................S. J. Cross
Wesley and Ohio Falls,
(A. J. Oster)
Leavenworth................F. T. Johnson

Leavenworth Ct.....(William Glosson)
Tower, Ind.
Little York..............(S. S. Spaulding)
Mauckport................... D. R. Johnson
New Albany—
Centenary......... George Dalrymple
Circuit................(Norris Spurgeon)
Henryville, Ind.
DePauw Memorial.......R. A. Ulrey
Main Street...................J. H. Allen
Trinity...................W. C. Patrick
Wesley Chapel...............J. G. Sibson
New Middletown............(C. L. Rice)
Otisco........................ (D. T. Stevens)
Orleans...........................J. S. Godwin
Paoli ....H. D. Bassett
Pekin...........................(E. L. Moore)
Salem...........................N. S. Jeffrey
Sellersburg...................W. E. Watkins
Scottsburg..................... Ralph Ogan
Taswell.................. (William Hunter)
Utica...........................A. H. Rumbley
R.R., Charlestown, Ind.
West Baden and
Ames...........(Eugene Montgomery)

Seymour District

L. C. Jeffrey, D.S., Seymour, Ind.

Aurora ....C. C. Bonnell
Brownstown.....................L. S. Lovell
Brooksburg............. (Elva Stambush)
Butlerville.....................Edwin Kitt
Columbus ....E. R. Zaring
Courtland............. (William DeHart)
Cross Plains...............(H. L. Holden)
Crothersville.................B. K. Johnson
Delaware................(Royal Canfield)
Dillsboro...............R. E. McWilliams
Dupont.....................(W. H. Murray)
East Columbus.........(Marion Gatlin)
Elizabethtown.............(C. C. Brown)
Fairview................(A. E. Wingham)

Hanover..................(Grace M. Harris)
Madison, Ind.
Hartford.....................H. M. Church
R.R., Aurora, Ind.
Hartsville.....................E. E. Young
Holton.....................Ralph Blodgett
Hope.....................Euphrates Barrett
Kent .... (Walter Matney)
Lawrenceburg..............W. C. Calvert
Lawrenceburg Ct.......(E. N. McCoy)
Madison...........................C. R. Stout
Manchester..................William Wood
R.R., Aurora, Ind.
Milan ....Millard Brittingham
Moores Hill....................C. C. Good

Napoleon......................(J. M. Taylor)
Newbern..................(W. H. Minter)
    R.R., Columbus, Ind.
North Madison.............N. C. Pfeiffer
North Vernon..............A. L. Meredith
Ogilsville.................(Arthur Rogers)
    R. R., Columbus, Ind.
Osgood...........................E. N. Rosier
Patriot..........................A. L. Howard

Rising Sun.....................J. T. Redmon
Seymour.........................W. E. Brown
Taylorsville.................. Harry Smith
Vallonia.......................(W. F. Crane)
Vernon.......................(G. W. Speedy)
Versailles....................(G. A. Marsh)
Vevay and Moorefield.....Arthur Jean
Wilmington.................(E. J. Hewitt)

Vincennes District

R. H. Toole, D.S., Vincennes, Ind.

Alfordsville..................(D. P. Willis)
Asbury.....................(H. R. Burton)
    Ragsdale, Ind.
Bicknell......................E. E. Aldrich
Bruceville.....................R. W. Parsley
Burns City.................(O. W. Lynch)
Carlisle...................L. D. Youngblood
Cass............................(U. V. Faris)
Decker ....(John Sutch)
Dugger......................J. M. Pynchon
Elnora...........................W. M. Clark
Farmersburg..................C. L. Wilson
Glendale.......................P. S. Lewis
    Montgomery, R.R.
Graysville.......................J. E. Harbin
Hymera....................... E. G. Jann
Indian Springs.............(John Morris)
Loogootee..........................O. M. Deal
Merom...................... (Guy Johnson)
Monroe City.............Edward Dawson
New Lebanon..................O. E. Killion
Oaktown ....(R. W. Robling)
Odon ....H. H. Sheldon
Otwell............................ James Todd

Petersburg..............A. C. McCullough
Petersburg Ct..............(F. Stoelting)
Pimento...........................C. F. Mahler
Plainsville.......................J. C. Foutz
Pleasantville..................(T. B. Avery)
Prairie Creek................(B. A. Eisman)
Prairieton..................C. L. Hughbanks
Riley...........................A. W. Shields
Sandborn..........................C. P. Hert
Shelburn......................F. P. Bedwell
Shoals........................Oscar Polhemus
Sullivan..........................W. E. Fisher
Union.................(George Thompson)
Vincennes—
    First Church..............W. H. Wylie
    North Church............B. E. Tryon
Wabash.......................(L. G. Miller)
    Decker, R. R.
Washington.....................S. L. Martin
Washington Ct..............(G. C. Peel)
Wheatland............W. H. Thompson
Winslow................(A. O. Bonecutter)
Youngstown.............(E. A. McBride)
    R.R.C., Terre Haute, Ind.

Special Appointments

H. W. Baldridge, Field Work Indiana Anti-Saloon League.
W. S. Bovard, Secretary Board of Education.
A. M. Couchman, Field Agent Preachers' Aid Society.
T. G. Duvall, Professor Osio Wesleyan University.
W. B. Farmer, Secretary Preachers' Aid Society.
E. E. Harper, President Evansville College.
E. B. Marlatt, Professor in Boston University.

L. C. Murr, Chaplain State Reformatory.
W. G. Parker, Professor in Evansville College.
Edwin Post, Professor in DePauw University.
G. M. Smith, Superintendent Methodist Hospitals.
J. L. Stout, Superintendent and Executive Secretary Methodist Children's Home.
C. B. Ware, Instructor of Religious Education, Epworth Seminary, Epworth, Ga.
Left without appointment to attend school—L. N. Abel, DePauw; J. J. Bailey, Boston; C. M. Bless, Garrett; J. L. Carter, Boston; R. L. Dove, Boston; F. E. Goodnough, Boston; F. R. Greer, Drew; R. M. Hays, Boston; R. S. Hendricks, Drew; C. S. Kendall, Boston; A. L. Lewis, DePauw; Guy Lowry, DePauw; H. G. Lytle, Boston; F. A. McDaniel, Garrett; E. M. McKown, Boston; G. K. Morelan, Columbia; H. R. Page, Boston; A. B. Parrett, Garrett; S. M. Riggle, Drew; W. A. Riggs, DePauw; H. F. Robbins, Boston; F. M. Sander, Evansville; N. I. Schoolfield, DePauw; J. M. Shaw, Boston; M. H. Webb, Boston; W. T. Wilson, Garrett.

Retired Ministers

W. L. Alexander, J. W. Allen, Jno. Asher, C. E. Bacon, O. E. Badger, A. R. Beach, R. D. Biven, J. A. Breeden, W. H. Brightmire, J. H. Carnes, E. M. Chambers, George Cochran, W. B. Collins, W. T. Davis, D. W. Denney, N. F. Denny, C. W. Dobson, J. H. Doddridge, Frank Edinborough, J. T. Edwards, W. J. Ellis, Grant Ferguson, H. O. Frazier, C. G. Fritsche, J. H. Furry, S. B. Grimes, H. W. Hargett, C. E. Hester, James Hixson, W. H. Howerton, J. M. D. Hudelson, M. B. Hyde, Allen Kenworthy, H. N. King, Lewis King, L. S. Knotts, E. D. C. Koeth, J. B. Lathrop, C. W. Maupin, J. P. Maupin, B. A. May, W. H. McDowell, J. F. McGregor, G. S. McKee, W. S. McMichael, G. F. McNaughton, L. D. Moore, S. A. Morrow, Alonzo Murphy, W. B. Niles, S. S. Penrod, J. L. Perry, M. L. Peyton, C. H. Pinnick, F. C. Raaf, C. S. Racy, John Ragle, Joseph Rawlins, Samuel Reid, J W. Robinson, S. J. Shake, J. L. Sims, J. H. Strain, W. F. Taylor, W. R. Thom, D. L. Thomas, E. O. Thomas, J. L. Vallow, B. T. VanCleave, J. A. Ward, J. S. Washburn, S. L. Welker, W. M. Whitsitt, C. S. Whitted, C. N. Willson, C. D. Wilson, E. L. Wimmer, T. W. Winkler, E. H. Wood, W. D. Woods, W. O. Wykoff.

Supernumeraries

C. T. Alexander, C. C. Brown, R. E. Coleman, E. A. Fiddler, W. R. Halstead, R. C. Todd, G. H. Reibold, Monroe Vayhinger, T. K. Willis.

NORTH INDIANA CONFERENCE APPOINTMENTS

Corrected to Date by D. V. Williams, Secretary.

Fort Wayne District

W. W. Wiant, D.S., Fort Wayne, Ind.

Angola...................W. E. Hogan	Huntertown.....................N. E. Smith
Arcola....................H. V. Cummins	Leo....................................I. L. Pusey
Ashley...................W. M. Hollopeter	Monroe............................E. M. Foster
Auburn...................G. E. Hubbartt	Monroeville......................J. F. Lutey
Auburn Circuit...........(Earl Clayton)	Montpelier....................Edward Antle
Blackford and Oakland	New Haven.................Thomas Davies
...............................(Glenn Bryan)	Orland...................(R. A. Shumaker)
Bluffton...................... W. W. Martin	Ossian...............................G. A. Snider
Bluffton Circuit (Homer Studebaker)	People's Chapel........(K. A. Hawkins)
Bobo.............................H. E. Forbes	Pleasant Mills.....................A. E. Burk
Coesse ....D. K. Finch	Poneto.......................L. L. C. Wisner
Decatur.......................R. W. Stoakes	Prospect Circuit........ (Ralph Preston)
Decatur Circuit................J. F. Blocker	Ray and Jones.................R. S. Brown
Flint.......................(To be supplied)	St. Joe and Taylor....(E. H. Hartman)
Fort Wayne—	Spencerville.................(T. J. Cotton)
First Church..............C. B. Croxall	Woodburn.............(George F. Crowe)
Forest Park.................A. R. Sanks	York....................(H. H. McMurtrey)
Fort Wayne Ct...........H. T. Shady	
Simpson.......................O. T. Martin	**RETIRED MINISTERS**
St. Paul.....................H. A. Davis	
Trinity....................H. R. Carson	M. C. Pittenger.........................Coesse
Waynedale.................C. G. Adams	C. A. Hunt.................Riverside, Cal.
Wayne Street........R. R. Detweiler	E. E. Wright....................Fort Wayne
Fremont........................H. A. Kirk	L. M. Krider....................Auburn
Garrett........................B. M. Bechdolt	A. S. Preston.................Angola, R. D.
Geneva .... N. P. Barton	Edwin Dickson ....Huntertown
Geneva Circuit............... G. F. Osbun	C. M. Hollopeter ....Warsaw
Hamilton.......................C. M. Bacon	D. H. Guild,
Harlan...........................E. P. White	Ft. Wayne, 1612 N. Anthony Blvd.
Hoagland......................A. L. Weaver	E. J. Maupin ....Bluffton
Hudson .... A. E. Scotten	

Goshen District

C. H. Smith, D.S., Goshen, Ind.

Albion.....................J. O. Hochstedler	Butler...................................J. R. Stelle
Avilla............................J. E. Lawshe	Corunna............................H. W. Park
Bourbon..................C. C. Wischmeier	Elkhart—
Bourbon Circuit.........B. F. Hornaday	Simpson .... V. L. Clear
Bristol............................L. M. Hile	St. Paul.................Charles Tinkham

Trinity.....................F. E. Fribley
Etna Green.....................J. W. Gibson
Goshen—
   First Church............H. L. Overdeer
   St. Mark's ....R. Godwin
Goshen Circuit..........(To be supplied)
Howe.....................E. E. Kauffman
Inwood.....................R. J. Johnson
Kendallville.....................R. J. Burns
Kimmel.....................E. J. Glendenning
Lagrange.....................F. H. Cremean
Leesburg.....................D. V. Williams
Ligonier.....................C. W. Anderson
Middlebury.....................F. A. LeMaster
Millford.....................F. R. Hill

Mishawaka—
   East ....H. M. Thrasher
   First.....................C. G. Yeomans
Nappanee.....................C. A. McPheeters
New Paris and
   Benton.....................R. J. Hutsinpiller
North Webster..........Arlington Singer
Osceola.....................F. D. Wilde
Pierceton.....................Sherman Powell

South Milford............F. A. Armstrong
Stroh.....................(Glen Dillingham)
Syracuse.....................J. H. Royer
Tippecanoe.....................C. H. Jennings
Topeka.....................E. E. DeWitt
Valentine ....(Ora Brock)
Wakarusa ....G. A. P. Jewell
Warsaw.....................J. T. Bean
Waterloo.....................H. E. Wright
Wawaka.....................(Kenneth Yost)
Wolcottville and
   Rome City.............Thurman Mott

SUPERNUMERARIES
S. B. Stookey.....................Elkhart

RETIRED MINISTERS
J. S. Cain.....................Warsaw
F. M. Kemper............San Diego, Cal.
E. L. Semans.....................Warsaw
C. E. White.....................Elkhart
F. M. Stone.....................Indianapolis
M. F. Stright.....................Gary
A. L. Lamport.............Burbank, Cal.
T. M. Guild.................Winona Lake
Somerville Light.....................Bristol

Logansport District
L. C. Bentley, D.S., Kokomo, Ind.

Amboy.....................(D. M. Church)
Anoka and Bethel......Claude Garrison
   R. D., Logansport.
Arcadia.....................C. G. Cook
Atlanta.....................L. F. Ulmer
Boxley—Salem............H. W. Mohler
   R. D., Sheridan.
Bunker Hill.....................W. B. Fallis
Center—Nevada.......Lewis J. Runion
Cicero.....................E. J. Magor
Converse.....................O. J. Beardsley
Denver-Chili.....................Edgar Moore
Ekin and Shiloh.............Ross Jackson
Elwood.....................H. C. Harman
   South Side Church.......Wayne Eller
Forest.....................E. A. Bunner
Frankton.....................J. H. Runkle
Galveston.....................C. A. Byrt
Gilead.....................J. R. Elson
Goldsmith.....................C. E. Dunlap

Greentown.....................E. L. Gates
Hillisburg.....................(Tom Stout)
Hobbs and Aroma..........C. W. Myers
Kempton-Scircleville ....J. M. Pynchon
Kokomo—
   Beamer.....................R. L. Wilson
      J. A. Patterson
   Grace.....................J. W. Potter
   Main Street..........Benjamin Kendall
   Trinity and Parr
      Memorial............Merrill L. Davis
   Kokomo Circuit..........O. A. Trabue
Lincoln.....................V. O. Vernon
Logansport—
   Broadway ....M. C. Wright
   Market Street..........H. A. P. Homer
   Wheatland.....................S. L. Yoder
Macy ....S. I. Zechiel

Mexico..................H. M. McMurray
Miami..................F. W. Launer
Peru....................A. H. Backus
Richland..............C. L. Schwartz
Roann-Paw Paw..........M. C. Morrow
Russiaville............C. W. Montgomery
Santa Fe..............F. S. Burns
Sharpsville............R. W. Graham
Sheridan..............E. R. Garrison
Somerset..............A. D. Burkett
Tipton................J. C. White
Twelve Mile..........G. W. Bailor
Walton................J. H. Richardson

West Middleton Ct...........C. L. Rees
Windfall..................J. S. Newcombe

SUPERNUMERARIES

J. M. Jordan..........................Kokomo
J. A. Patterson.............Battle Ground

RETIRED MINISTERS

C. H. Brown......................... Kokomo
G. E. Garrison....................Galveston
H. E. McFarlane.................Russiaville
J. M. B. Reeves....................Converse
A. J. Duryee...................... Galveston
F. J. Speckien....................Kokomo
J. J. Fred............................Sharpsville

Muncie District

W. T. Arnold, D.S., Muncie, Ind.

Albany..................C. M. Fawns
Albany Circuit..........(Herbert Perry)
Alexandria..............A. F. Hogan
Alexandria Circuit......(Earl Leonard)
Anderson—
  First.....................F. A. Hall
  Grace.................. O. A. Knox
  Indiana Avenue.........D.A.J. Brown
  Noble Street.................P. B. Smith
  Park Place.................. J. W. Rose
Beal's Chapel and
  Strawtown................(H. C. Taska)
Blountsville...................Maurice Jones
Carmel Ct.....................O. P. Van Y
Daleville Circuit..........R. M. Criswell
DeSoto..................G. W. Thomas
Eaton....................G. V. Saunders
Fishers..................J. E. Jensen
Fortville.................A. J. Armstrong
Gaston....................J. W. Fox
Hartford City—
  Grace................L. G. Jacobs
  Grant Street...................Lee Wilson
Ingalls Ct.................(L. D. Albright)
Jolietville Ct...............L. B. Sharp
  P. O. Westfield.
Lapel.....................E. J. Wickersham
Matthews.....................R. E. Davison
Middletown..............G. L. Conway

Muncie—
  Avondale.................B. H. Franklin
  High Street...................C. H. King
  Madison Street.............G. H. Myers
  Normal City..........W. E. Pittenger
  Whiteley..........M. B. Graham
New Burlington..............(C. A. Mills)
  R.D., Muncie.
Noblesville.................M. O. Lester
Noblesville Circuit.......C. B. Thomas
Pendleton................Dale C. Beatty
Perkinsville Ct..........(Claudius Pyle)
  R.D., Anderson.
Rigdon...................C. W. Fisk
  R.D., Elwood.
Selma..................J. B. Sparling
Shideler..................F. A. Shipley
Summitville................W. E. Loveless
Union....................(Jesse House)
Westfield..................J. W. Reynolds
Yorktown.................W. E. Hamilton
Zion and Shiloh................K. Maynard

RETIRED MINISTERS

W. W. Brown.......................Muncie
J. P. Chamness........................Muncie
C. E. Line..........401 Harvard Place,
                    Indianapolis, Ind.
J. H. McNary......................... Albany

W. H. Pierce................Selma
R. S. Reed................Muncie, R.D. 5
Lewis Reeves................Hartford City
J. A. Ruley......1000 E. Washington
                 Street, Muncie
L. A. Sevits ....Albany
W. F. Walker................Springfield, Ill.

J. E. Williams................Indianapolis
J. Z. Barrett..............Bradentown, Fla.
J. F. Bailey........................Greencastle
E. B. Westhafer,
         New Philadelphia, Ohio
E. H. Taylor......................Alexandria

Richmond District

F. F. Thornburg, D.S., Richmond, Ind.

Cambridge City..........W. H. Harrison
Centerville........................A. K. Love
Charlottesville..................(J. W. Cox)
Chester and Webster......(E. L. Miller)
  R.D., Richmond.
Dublin........................ (Ewart Talley)
Dunkirk........................A. E. Leese
Economy........................A. C. Hoover
Farmland........................S. F. Harter
Farmland Circuit......(To be supplied)
Fountain City............(S. E. Carruth)
Greenfield................W. B. Freeland
Hagerstown................ E. D. Imler
Kennard....................(A. M. Taylor)
Knightstown..................J. H. Palmer
Lewisville....................J. O. Campbell
Losantville............... (To be supplied)
Lynn ....E. E. Lutes
Markleville..................S. G. Jennings
Maxwell.................... Gail Davis
McCordsville................Julius Pfeiffer
Millgrove....................J. H. Brown
Modoc........................E. F. Landrey
New Castle—
  Centenary ....D. B. Jennings
  First................L. W. Kemper
Parker........................E. L. Jones
Pennville....................J. A. Land
Philadelphia.................. (E. Lawshe)
Portland ....E. E. Trippeer

Portland Circuit..............(D. Liggett)
Redkey..........................U. S. Hartley
Redkey Circuit............(G. G. Girton)
Richmond—
  Central ....J. I. Jones
  Trinity........................P. Polhemus
Ridgeville........................C. E. Smith
Salamonia......................(Ray Noland)
Saratoga........................... H. L. Liddle
Shirley..................... (To be supplied)
Spiceland........................E. S. McKee
Union Chapel.......... (Morris D. James)
Union City..................T. S. Haddock
Whitewater and
  Middleboro..................C. A. Cloud
  Richmond, R.D.
Wilkinson......................E. C. Fisher
Williamsburg..................J. M. Stewart
Willow Branch..........C. R. Stockinger
Winchester..................P. E. Greenwalt
Winchester Circuit.........W. P. Thorn

RETIRED MINISTERS

S. Billheimer....................Hagerstown
F. G. Browne, Indianapolis Y.M.C.A.
R. T. Laslie..............Hardinsburg, Ky.
L. P. Pfeifer....................Greenfield
M. S. Marble.................. Indianapolis
J. O. Bills....................Lewisville
J. S. Phillips......................Star City
G. W. Martin........................Albany

Wabash District

U. S. A. Bridge, D.S., Wabash, Ind.

Akron............................R. H. Wehrly
Andrews..........................S. H. Caylor
Bippus..........................E. W. Hamilton
Churubusco.....................A. W. Pugh
Churubusco Circuit.........F. S. Young
Claypool..........................T. B. Morris
Columbia City.....................H. Boase
Etna..............................E. J. Hults
    Columbia City, R.D. 9.
Fairmount..........................C. A. Hile
Gas City................J. H. Stephenson
Huntington...................J. F. Edwards
Jonesboro..............B. D. Nysewander
LaFontaine.....................D. C. Souder
Lagro........................K. R. Thompson
Larwill..........................J. C. Graham
Lincolnville......................H. H. Harris
    Wabash, R.D. 6.

Marion—
    First....................... F. K. Dougherty
    Grace..........................H. C. Powell
    Highland Ave..........G. A. Tennant
    Home Park....(W. H. Baumbaugh)
        Marion R.D. 11.
    Ninth Street.............. V. E. Stoner
Markle.............................A. P. Teter
Mentone.......................W. O. Power
Morris Chapel.............(Travis Purdy)
    Marion, R.D. 8.
Mount Etna..................J. W. Borders
    Huntington, R.D. 7.
North Manchester..........R. C. Plank

Point Isabel................E. H. Saunders
    Swayzee, R.D. 2.
Roanoke...................C. W. Shoemaker
Roll...........................(C. E. Parsons)
Silver Lake.................E. H. Kennedy
Sims...........................(H. P. Young)
South Whitley.................O. C. Bogue
Swayzee..........................C. S. Miller
Sweetser......................A. G. Simmons
Uniondale.......................W. L. Hall
Upland........................E. E. Franklin
Vanburen.......................J. L. Gillard
Wabash—
    First.............................J. F. Porter
    Middle Street.............C. B. Sweeney
    Wabash Street.........E. B. Megenity
Warren................... A. C. Wischmeier
Warsaw Circuit..............Garry Browne

RETIRED MINISTERS

J. W. Bowen............................Marion
J. W. Cain....................DeLand, Fla.
H. A. Ewell..................Dayton, Ohio
J. W. Tillman........North Manchester
G. B. Work
    356 Tulane Road, Columbus, Ohio
W. E. Murray................. Huntington
C. H. Murray......................Andrews
J. L. Murr.............Greenfield, R.D. 6
O. V. L. Harbour.................Laketon
J. L. Sturgell..................Canton, Ill.
Henry Lacy,
            1814 Clay St., Ft. Wayne
David Wells .... Marion

SPECIAL APPOINTMENTS

R. J. Wade, Executive Secretary World Service.
C. U. Wade, General Secretary Preachers' Aid Society.
H. B. Gough, Professor DePauw University.
W. W. Sweet, Professor Theological Seminary, Chicago University.
W. E. McPheeters, Professor Lawrence College.
B. S. Hollopeter, Corresponding Secretary Methodist Memorial Home.
R. A. Morrison, Financial Secretary Taylor University.
J. W. Oborn, Stewardship Evangelist World Service Commission.

Earle Naftzger, Conference Evangelist.
R. W. Rogers, Chaplain U. S. Army.
R. V. Johnson, Field Secretary Board of Temperance and Public Morals.
Walter W. Krider, Missionary to Japan.
O. W. French, Missionary in Korea.
F. P. Morris, Professor Systematic Theology, Asbury College.
Leroy Huddleston, Field Secretary Anti-Saloon League.

The following were left without appointment to attend school: John S. Denbo, John H. Collier, Clarence Ferris, J. W. Reeves, R. A. Fenstermacher, G. T. Oborn, A. C. Rehme, H. J. Keiser, L. M. Bonner, B. T. Osborne, R. J. Fleming, Paul L. Hargitt, W. L. Whitaker, R. W. Newell.

E. M. Dunbar, Leave of Absence.
J. J. Fischer, Solicitor Methodist Institutions.
John Paul, President Taylor University.
H. A. Clugston, Wesley Foundation, Denver, Colorado.
B. T. Osborne, S. Wilmore, Kentucky.
L. M. Bonner, S. Madison, New Jersey.
J. O. Powell, Conference Evangelist.

In His Presence

"They cannot be where God is not—on any sea or shore."

JOHN T. SCULL, SR.	FESTUS A. STEELE	CHARLES E. DISBRO
CHARLES CURTIS EDWARDS	HARRY AKNDREWS KING	JOHN W. DUNCAN
MADISON SWADENER		BENJAMIN F. IVEY
OWEN HENRY CLARK	WILLIAM P. McKINSEY	JOHN WESLEY FLINT

NORTHWEST INDIANA CONFERENCE

Corrected to date by F. O. Fraley, Secretary.

Crawfordsville District

Otto T. Martin, D.S., Crawfordsville, Ind.

Attica................................T. L. Stovall
Bringhurst....................(F. S. Martin)
Brownsburg.................G. E. Tremaine
Burlington ....John Walton
Clark's Hill-Mechanicsburg,
                    (L. N. Abel)
Colfax............................L. L. Bickett
Covington...................... J. B. Johnson
Crawfordsville—
  First....................Guy O. Carpenter
  Trinity......................A. L. Miller
Darlington-Potato Creek, ...
                        E. M. Kuonen
Flackville-Bethel............U. G. Abbott
Flora................................S. C. Rogers
Frankfort.........................F. L. Hovis
Hillsboro-Waynetown........E. F. Prevo
Jackson Heights (P.O. West Point,
  R. F. D.) ....C. C. Pearce
Jamestown....................Geo. B. Jones
Kirklin-Lane's Chapel (W. M. Krider)
Ladoga-New Market........Carl Martine
Lebanon..............................H. P. Ivey
Linden-Kirkpatrick........R. W. Michel
Lizton-Advance................V. E. Fruits
Mace-New Ross (P.O. Crawfords-

ville, R.F.D.).........(Geo. L. Hartz)
Michigantown-Morris Chapel.........
                        J. W. Knight
Moran-Killmore...............C. P. Martin
Mulberry...................... E. V. Claypool
New Richmond..............W. H. Bleam
Pittsboro-Elmdale........ (Merrill Ivey)
Pence's............................. L. E. Morris
Pine Village-Rainsville, J. C. Whitson
Romney.................. (Clarence Ferris)
Rossville..........................O. R. Mason
Stockwell..........................A. W. Smith
Thorntown..................... R. W. Knight
Veedersburg-Salem.........C. H. Leeson
Waveland-Russellville.......F. J. Beisel
Wesley-Roberts (P.O., 34 N. 26th
  St., Lafayette.........(V. C. Rogers)
West Lebanon-State Line,...............
                        R. W. Sturm
Whitestown-Pleasant View-Cler-
  mont.......................... J. A. Gardner
Williamsport...................C. C. Harold
Wingate-Newton............G. P. Burdon
West Point-Bethel....W. D. Archibald
Yountsville-Alamo....(George Beatty)
Zionsville-Salem ....W. M. Nicely

Greencastle District

A. T. Briggs, D.S., Greencastle, Ind.

Avon (P.O., Danville, R.F.D.) ......
                    (W. C. Aye)
Bainbridge-New Maysville (P. O.
  Greencastle) ....(G. L. Clore)
Bellmore-Morton............H. J. Barnaby
Ben Davis (P. O., Indianapolis, R.
  R. O.) ....A. L. Brandenburg

Brazil:
  First................................ R. B. Kern
  Epworth-Peniel (P. O., Green-
    castle............(Medford E. Maxwell)
Brick Chapel-Fillmore-Wesley (P.
  O., Greencastle) ....
                (Gordon Chapman)
Carbon...................(Rockwell Smith)

Clayton (P. O., Brazil)................
.... (Hugh McGlasson)
Clinton:
First................Benjamin Rist
Fairview Park (P. O., Clinton)
.... Lynn Bates
Coatesville-Amo ....R. W. Fish
Dana................(C. H. Thomas)
Danville................J. A. Lord
Greencastle................C. H. Taylor
Indianapolis:
Riverside Park (1228 Burdsall
Parkway)................R. M. Selle
Robindale (P. O., Greencastle)
...................(N. Schofield)
Speedway Blvd., (964 N. Tibbs
St.)................ Clyde Lininger
St. Paul's (2916 Rader St.)........
................Elmer Jones
West Park-Bridgeport (P. O. In-
dianapolis, 3465 N. Dearborn St.)
.... Joseph Edwards
Kingman-Bloomingdale ......
...................(A. H. Roahrig)
Knightsville-Bethel (P.O., Green-
castle)................(Franklin Cole)
Lena-Sharon (P. O., Greencastle)..
.... (Earl Ferguson)
Montezuma-Mecca-Linebarger ......
................A. L. Vermillion
North Salem................W. W. Clouse
Newport-Hillsdale....O. L. Chivington
Perrysville................(E. T. Miles)
Plainfield................ Israel Hatton
Reelsville-Harmony (P. O., Green-
castle)................(William Ellis)

Roachdale-Raccoon (P. O., Bloom-
ington, Ind., 701 Atwater St.,)
.... (Paul Vietzke)
Rockville................C. M. McClure
Rosedale-Bridgeton......J. M. Williams
Sanford-Catlin (P.O., Greencastle)
.... (Odus Mitchell)
Seelyville (P.O., Greencastle).........
................(Lowell J. Smith)
Staunton-Glenn Ayr (P. O., Green-
castle)................(Robert Reed)
Smith Park-Bethesda (P. O., Rose-
dale, R.F.D.)........(Hugh VanLieu)

Terre Haute—
Fourth Ave., (1125 N. 4th St.,)
................W. B. Warriner
Grace (1422 North Avenue)......
................(T. B. Reed)
Lafayette Avenue, 1129 N. 8th
St.,)................(William Daniels)
Liberty Avenue (2420 Sycamore
St.)................(E. J. Peters)
Maple Avenue (2122 N. 11th)..
................J. E. Porter
Methodist Temple (315 N. 7th)
................L. M. Lounsbury
Montrose (1600 College St.).........
................H. E. Moore
North Terre Haute-Burnett-Rose
Hill (P.O., Terre Haute, R. R.
E)................ (D. E. Reed)
Trinity (1115 N. 14th St.)........
................W. N. Whear
West Terre Haute (P.O. Brazil)
................(R. B. Stewart)

Lafayette District

John J. Wilson, D.S., Lafayette, Ind.

Ambia-Talbot................L. E. Watson
Barkley (P.O. Rensselaer)............
................Roy J. Hicks
Battle Ground................H. M. Braun
Boswell................J. P. Alford
Brook................C. C. Jordan
Brookston................ H. F. Pearson

Buck Creek (P.O., Y.M.C.A., La-
fayette)................(Avery Moore)
Burnettsville................ (Clinton Polen)
Camden................ (Frank Collier)
Clymers (P. O., Forrest) ....
.... Kenneth Cohee
Dayton................ P. A. Reisen

Delphi ....O. P. Manker
Fowler.........................S. P. Reakes
Francesville.....................C. E. Beebee
Goodland.......................T. A. Griffin
Idaville.............(Charles L. Rinehart)
Kentland......................J. E. McCloud
Kewanna................. W. L. Hargrave
Lafayette:
   Congress St.............F. G. Howard
   St. Paul.....................G. S. Reedy
   Trinity.....................T. F. Williams
   First-West Lafayette ...M. C. Hunt
   Associate................H. D. Bollinger
Leiters Ford...............H. L. Adams
Lowell.......................V. V. Hackley
Lucerne..................... D. E. Noland
Medaryville..................S. A. Bender
Monon........................L. H. Ice
Monticello.................J. G. Campbell

Montmorenci.................A. A. Dunlavy
Morocco...........................J. W. Niell
Mount Ayr...............(L. A. Willsey)
Otterbein.................. Earl Heimburger
Oxford..................A. E. Dougherty
Raub, (P. O., Kentland) ....
   ....J. E. McCloud
Remington...................... L. P. Green
Rensselaer................... Claude Young
Reynolds-Yeoman,
   ....(Delos W. O'Brien)
Richland Center........(Fred L. Leeper)
Rochester.....................R. H. Crowder
Royal Center...................W. V. Day
Star City.....................P. B. Burleigh
Stidham Memorial (P. O., West
   Lafayette) ....O. F. Hall
Winamac................... A. C. Northrop
Wolcott....................Stanley S. Hall

South Bend District

Bert D. Beck, D.S., South Bend, Ind.

Argos...............W. B. Collier
Bethel-Tefft (P.O., Garrett Dorm.,
   Evanston, Ill.) (Harry Illingworth)
Chesterton-Burdick.........A. E. Bagby
Crown Point.............M. H. Appleby
Culver.....................V. B. Servies
DeMonte-Kniman ....
   ....(Walter W. Wilson)
East Chicago (4710 Baring Ave.)
   ....B. R. Nesbit
Gary:
   First (564 Madison St.) ....
   ....(W. F. Switzer)
   Assistant (732 Harrison St.) ......
   .... W. F. Switzer
   Grace (3879 Washington St.) ....
   ....W. K. Ingalls
Griffith ....(Joyce Bailey)
Hamlet...................A. H. Lawrence
Hammond:
   Centenary (93 Sheffield Avenue)
   ....C. N. McBrayer
   First (38 Webb St.) ......C. C. Ford

Hyde Park (1212 Harrison) .....
   ....H. V. Deale
Hanna...............Raymond Earle
Hebron.............. Richard Pengilly
Hobart....................C. F. Craig
Indiana Harbor (3505 Grand Blvd.)
   ....W. A. Griest
Knox....................G. A. Trodie
LaCrosse...................(Mark E. Smith)
Lakeville...................J. E. Dean
LaPorte...................A. H. Kenna
Leroy (P.O., Garrett Dorm., Ev-
   anston, Ill.) ....(F. A. McDaniels)
Maple Grove-Sumption Prairie (Gar-
   rett Dorm., Evanston, Ill.) ....
   .... (Russell Oberlin)
Merrillville............(Stanley S. McKee)
Michigan City (509 Spring St.) ....
   ....F. O. Fraley
New Carlisle - Hamilton - Maple
   Grove....................C. V. Bigler
North Judson..............H. L. McBride
North Liberty...............W. C. Evers
Ober......................(M. J. Griffin)
Plymouth..................E. W. Strecker

Poplar Grove........(J. C. Brumbaugh)
Salem (P.O., Garrett Dorm., Ev-
anston, Ill.).............C. C. Rockwell
Rolling Prairie-Lamb's Chapel (P.
O., Garrett Dorm., Evanston,
Ill.) ....(C. M. Bless)
South Bend:
Epworth (929 Olive St.)...........
...................................C. A. Brown
Assistant..................G. W. Switzer
First (315 N. Main St.)...........
...................................A. E. Monger
Grace (111 E. Tutt St.)...........
................................E. M. Ellsworth
Lowell Heights (511 N. Francis
St.)..............................M. C. Bishop
River Park (913 S. 7th St.)........
...............................R. Ross-Shannon

St. Paul's Memorial (1007 W.
Colfax Ave.)............P. L. Benedict
Stull Memorial (2425 So. Michi-
gan St.)...................F. H. Longwell
Trinity (921 Cleveland Ave.)....
................................R. O. Kimberlin
South Bend Circuit (R. R. 5,
South Bend)............(P. T. Shields)
Valpaiaiso....................F. R. Briggs
Walkerton..................C. B. Stanforth
Wanatah (P.O., Valparaiso).........
............................(J. W. Moreland)
Waterford (P.O., Michigan City)..
...............................(A. W. Wood)
Westville-Door Village, C. V. Roush
Wheatfield (To be supplied.)
Wheeler-McCool......(Karl L. Darkey)
Whiting (307 Sheridan Ave.)........
...............................A. S. Warriner

Special Appointments

E. C. Wareing, Editor Western Christian Advocate.
L. R. Eckardt, Professor DePauw University, Greencastle.
S. B. Town, Treasurer, DePauw University, Greencastle.
E. S. Shumaker, State Superintendent Anti-Saloon League.
O. F. Hall, Professor Purdue University, West Lafayette.
F. F. Hargrave, Professor Purdue University, West Lafayette.
C. D. Royse, Counsellor in Finance, Indianapolis Area.
B. E. Kirkpatrick, Secretary Dept. Epworth League, Board of Education.
H. L. Davis, Executive Secretary Preachers' Aid Society.
B. E. Horn, Superintendent Friendship House, Gary.
H. R. DeBra, Dept. of Evangelism, Board of Home Missions.
G. H. Black, Evangelist, Greencastle.
H. O. Enwall, Professor Florida State University, Gainesville, Fla.
H. C. Riley, Methodist Hospital, Indianapolis.
Henry Ostrom, Evangelist, Greencastle.
N. F. Forsythe, Board of Education.
A. W. Wood, Chaplain Indiana State Prison, Michigan City.
U. G. Leazenby, Field Agent Methodist Hospital, Gary.
William D. Schermerhorn, Professor Garrett Biblical Institute, Evans-
ton, Illinois.
Charles R. Lizenby, Indiana Council Religious Education, Indianapolis.
Lester M. Jones, Professor DePauw University, Greencastle.
Carroll D. Hildebrand, Professor DePauw University, Greencastle.
Left without Appointment to attend School: Clarence H. Loveland, Ir-
win G. Paulsen, E. Duane Thistlethwaite, Lofton S. Wesley, Cloyd V. Gustaf-
son, Van W. Hinckley, Martin Rist, Homer H. Cloud.

Retired Ministers

A. V. Babbs, William Brandon, W. H. Broomfield, H. N. Calton, J. F. Clearwaters, J. B. Combs, G. F. Cramer, P. C. Curnick, G. E. Deuel, W. N. Dunn, T. J. Everett, A. M. Hagenbook, C. L. Harper, W. H. Hickman, J. H. Kevan, A. M. Mahaffie, W. E. McKenzie, J. B. McNary, H. N. Ogden, E. G. Pelley, C. W. Postill, T. J. Reder, O. B. Rippetoe, W. B. Rippetoe, J. P. Shagley, J. E. Sidebottom, C. B. Smith, L. S. Smith, C. O. Smock, W. J. Stewart, G. R. Streeter, W. F. Switzer, W. I. Taylor, J. N. Thompson, C. E. Tinkham, H. C. Weston, A. W. Wood, J. H. Worrall.

Supernumeraries

F. H. Collier, D. Tillotson, O. R. South, S. W. Goss, A. D. Wagner, G. E. Francis, F. W. Harlow, G. V. Morris.

SOUTHERN ILLINOIS CONFERENCE

Corrected to date by Geo. R. Goodman, Secretary.

Carbondale District

W. M. Brown, D.S., Carbondale, Ill.

Anna................................B. H. Batson
Brookport....................A. H. Reynolds
Cairo................................A. R. Ransom
Carbondale—
    First........................W. P. MacVey
    Grace..........................S. D. Berst
Carterville............E. E. Montgomery
Chester........................T. C. Stokes
Coulterville..................L. M. Leyerle
Crab Orchard................E. H. Purdy
Creal Springs................T. A. Shaffer
Cypress............................L. F. Vise
DuBois......................(A. N. Norris)
DuQuoin................W. D. Richardson
Eddyville..........................J. R. Reid
Elizabethtown............Ernest Connett
Elkville......................G. W. Hanks
Ellis Grove....................S. S. Smith
Golconda......................O. C. Trail
Herrin........................F. W. Pimlott
Johnson City..................J. H. Davis

Jonesboro......................H. M. Fish
Joppa............................(T. J. Isaacs)
Karnak..........................A. N. Hicks
Makanda..................(Bruce Ramsey)
Marion........................J. W. Cummins
Metropolis....................W. I. Terhune
Mound City..............Lawrence Smith
Mounds........................H. B. Shoaff
Murphysboro..............Robert Morris
New Burnside............(John Sutton)
Pinckneyville..................J. S. Dever
Pittsburg................W. A. Berneking
Reevesville..................G. A. Dunn
Royalton and Energy, Paul B. Brown
Steelville..................W. E. Browning
Sparta....................W. H. McPherson
Thebes and Olive Branch,
                  T. A. Martin
Ullin............................S. A. Morgan
Vergennes....................Elmer Smith
Vienna........................J. M. Clayton
Villa Ridge and Elco, Chas. Atchison

Centralia District

C. B. Whiteside, D.S., Centralia, Ill.

Alma................................C. C. Mays
Altamont........................O. B. Kinsey
Ashley............................F. E. Harris
Beaucoup....................W. G. Wigham
Beaver Creek................(Glen Sharp)
Beecher City........(E. B. Blankenship)
Brownstown................G. S. Hammons
Carlyle..........................L. W. Cralley

Centralia—
    Central City........Ernest Shepherd
    First............................M. H. Loar
    Second............................E. W. Fox

Coffeen and Vera, (Lebanon P. O.)
                  (A. D. Hagler)
Donnellson and Panama,
                J. W. Gammon
Effingham....................T. B. Sowers
Farina..........................C. H. Spragg
Fillmore and Van Burenburg,
                H. A. Tempel
Greenville—
    Centenary and Smithboro,
              (A. D. Hawley)
    First............................L. A. Magill

Herrick ....O. H. Young
Hoyleton and North Prairie,
                                Henry Idel
Huey ....Gail Hines
Irvington ....E. C. Phillips
Kinmundy ....E. G. Wininger
Litchfield ....C. C. Cullison
Marissa ....O. O. Maxfield
Mason ....(P. O. Anderson)
Moccasin ....(C. C. Yeck)
Mt. Olive ....C. C. Dawdy
Mulberry Grove ....J. F. Kapp
Nashville—
  First ....Owen Wright
  Wesley ....D. A. Tappmeyer

New Baden and Okawville,
                                F. C. Brown
Oakdale ....D. A. Tappmeyer
Pocahontas ....W. L. Rhein
Ramsey ....C. H. Carlton
St. Elmo ....C. L. Phifer
Salem ....J. E. Shafer
Shattuc, (Lebanon P. O.) F. C. Mery
Shobonier ....C. M. Miller
Sorento ....J. F. Glotfelty
Tilden ....S. Albrecht
Trenton ....H. N. Wills
Vandalia ....J. D. Shaddrick
Vernon ....(O. D. Mitzel)
Walnut Hill ....(Irvin Smith)
Watson ....(M. Condo)

East St. Louis District

W. H. Whitlock, D.S., East St. Louis, Ill.

Alton—
  First ....M. A. Souers
  Grace ....T. H. Roddey
  Main Street ....N. C. Henderson
Batchtown ....(J. T. Clower)
Belleville—
  Epworth ....(C. H. Starkey)
  First ....J. S. Cummins
  Jackson St. ....G. W. Humphrey
Bethalto and Fosterburg,
                        (Delbert Lacquement)
Brighton ....J. G. Korb
Bunker Hill—
  First ....Otto Horsley
  Schutz Memorial ....Wm. Schutz
Caseyville ....H. L. Metcalf
Callinsville ....W. H. Poole
Dorchester, (Lebanon P. O.)
                                (C. L. Allen)
East Alton ....(C. J. Harms)
East St. Louis—
  Alta Sita ....R. M. Stockton
  Bond Ave. and Settlement House,
                                W. D. Simmons
  First ....O. L. Markman
  St. Paul's ....L. S. McKown
  Signal Hill ....L. G. Beers
  State St. ....J. W. Webster

Edwardsville—
  Immaneul ....F. F. Otto
  St. John's ....J. G. Tucker
Elisah ....D. S. Gerlach
Freeburg and New Athens,
                                V. N. Gould
Gillespie ....E. U. Yates
Godfrey ....F. M. Hedger
Grafton ....C. J. Struebing
Granite City—
  Dewey Ave. ....Benj. J. Adams
  East Granite ....H. Y. Slaton
  Niedringhaus Memorial,
                                P. R. Glotfelty
  Zion ....D. Froeschle
Hamburg ....T. J. Wilson
Hartford and Wanda,
                                D. W. Hussong
Jerseyville ....J. B. Cummins
Kane ....C. W. Hall
Lebanon ....C. R. Yost
Madison ....A. A. Hagler
Mascoutah ....Carl Fritz
Medora ....T. O. Holley
O'Fallon ....(L. E. Morris)
Piasa and Fidelity, P. R. Glotfelty, Jr.
St. Jacob ....(Louis Head)
Shipman and Plainview, Ira E. Lutz

Staunton............................R. N. Kean
Troy and Glen Carbon, (Lebanon
P. O.) ....John Montgomery
Venice, (Lebanon P.O.),
          (E. J. Murdoch)

Waterloo (Lebanon P. O.,)
....(J. G. Dee)
Wood River..............O. F. Whitlock

Mt. Carmel District

C. L. Peterson, D.S., Mt. Vernon, Ill.

Albion......................C. D. Shumard
Benton...................... T. B. McClain
Bellmont......................Z. W. Story
Big Prairie...................R. O. Clements
Browns....................Angus Phillips
Bruce, (Crossville P.O.),
          (Claude Piland)
Carrier Mills...................J. H. Sharda
Carmi................W. J. Fahnestock
Centerville, (Grayville R.F.D.),
          Stephen Stanley
Christopher......................W. E. Bush
Crossville........................ Mayo Bowles
Dahlgren......................D. R. Luke
Eldorado—
  Beulah Heights....W. J. Westbrook
  First..............................J. R. Slaten
Enfield........................C. R. Wise
Equality...................F. C. Stelzriede
Galatia......................G. A. Phelps
Grayville...................S. A. Matthews
Harrisburg...................O. E. Connett
Ina................Raymond Richardson
Macedonia................. (J. T. Bryant)
Maunie......................J. W. Tucker

McLeansboro.................H. W. Smoot
Mill Shoals......................J. E. Lamb
Mt. Carmel......................M. C. Foltz
Mt. Vernon—
  Circuit..........................W. J. Leslie
  Epworth................. J. H. Davidson
  First........................ G. R. Goodman
  Wesley...................W. Clyde Bruce
Norris City....................C. M. Prince
Omaha...................... (Homer Young)
Opdyke........................ (J. A. Taylor)
Orient, (West Frankfort P.O.),
          C. S. Barnett
Ridgway........................O. R. Buess
Sesser............................ E. W. Barrett
Shawneetown.............. (J. C. Kinison)
Thompsonville.............Russell Heiney
Valier...................... (Hubert Hurley)
Waltonville..................H. C. Ingram
Wayne City............ (Homer Farthing)
West Frankfort—
  Central ....C. S. Tritt
  Epworth....................(S. N. Fisk)
  First..............................O. B. Allen
  Trinity..........................L. E. Page
Ziegler......................E. F. Williams

Olney District

Frank O. Wilson, D.S., Olney, Ill.

Allendale....................Marion Jackson
Bone Gap..........................J. N. Presley
Bridgeport......................J. B. Jones
Calhoun......................W. W. Ashby
Chauncy...................... (Lewis Jones)
Cisne................................Henry Heyer

Claremont....................C. B. Johnston
Clay City....................M. L. Watson
Dieterich...................... (J. P. Tucker)
Fairfield, Circuit............W. E. Shaffer
Fairfield, First.................J. M. Adams
Flat Rock......................C. H. Todd
Flora..............................J. B. Johnson

Friendsville........(C. H. Campbell)
    Mt. Carmel, R.F.D.
Geff..............................V. W. Corrie
Golden Gate................B. H. Cravens
Hutsonville.......................G. H. Hall
Iuka................F. W. Schwarzlose
Johnsonville.................James McNabb
Lawrenceville...........Ressho Robertson
Louisville........................J. L. Miller
Mt. Erie....................(W. C. Brumit)
Newton..........................E. T. Carroll
Noble...........................R. R. Howe
Oblong, Circuit................E. L. Lawler
Oblong, First.................L. W. Porter
Olney.........................W. E. Bennett

Palestine Circuit........(M. A. Sanders)
Palestine, First.................O. F. Culver
Pinkstaff ....E. H. Cissna
Robinson.......................J. H. Cudlipp
Rose Hill...................(W. S. Wilcox)
       Newton, Ill.
Sailor Springs...............(J. E. Owens)
St. Francesville................T. E. Harper
Sumner...........................W. M. Lane
West Salem.....................E. E. Linder
West Liberty................(Frank Staley)
Wheeler......................... Walter Fagan
Willow Hill................(J. D. Shouse)
       Newton, Ill.
Xenia.............................A. A. Ferrell

Special Appointments

Cameron Harmon, president; W. C. Walton and J. W. A. Kinison, professors in McKendree College.

David S. Wahl, field secretary McKendree College.

C. C. Hall, superintendent Methodist Orphanage.

C. L. Coleman, superintendent, and C. W. Hall, chaplain Old Folks' Home.

A. L. Shafer, agent Anti-Saloon League.

Conference Evangelists—E. O. Allen, W. E. Lamp.

Left Without Appointment to Attend One of Our Schools—W. L. Hanbaum, Emmet Hard, Ernest L. Mathis, O. R. Spreckelmeyer, M. J. Wahl, J. W. Walker.

Retired Ministers

Charles Atchison, John A. Bell, Charles B. Besse, C. E. Bovard, William R. Bradley, J. E. Burke, Greenlee Calvert, Theodore Cates, Lemuel Cramp, G. W. Dame, J. G. Dee, John Wesley DeWeese, W. W. Edwards, Z. J. Farmer, J. S. Hall, J. G. Harmon, Henry O. Hiser, Benjamin A. Hoar, J. T. Huffman, Willard Kiesling, J. C. Kinison, Lovell R. Mauk, Edward H. McKenzie, J. W. McNeill, H. L. Merrick, H. F. Miller, W. T. Morris, J. T. Murkin, C. A. Neumeyer, J. E. Nickerson, F. W. Schlueter, G. A. Seed, W. F. Sipfle, J. W. Smith, J. A. Taylor, F. M. Van Treese, J. P. Watson, G. M. Shitzell, W. S. Wilcox, Adam Yingst, Hiram H. Young.

Supernumeraries

D. W. Shipp, C. W. Smith, A. F. Zimmerman.

The Roll of Honor

Names of preachers in the conferences of Indianapolis Area translated to the Church Triumphant during the quadrennium nineteen twenty-four to twenty-eight:

INDIANA CONFERENCE

F. A. Guthrie	July 20, 1924
S. O. Dorsey	Nov. 6, 1924
F. E. Dugan	Dec. 8, 1924
John Royer	Dec. 22, 1924
M. S. Taylor	April 7, 1925
C. E. Ketcham	April 23, 1925
E. R. Vest	Oct. 25, 1925
C. C. Edwards	Jan. 2, 1926
G. W. Holmes	Feb. 2, 1926
J. T. Scull, Sr.	Feb. 6, 1926
F. A. Steele	April 20, 1926
H. L. Niles	May 21, 1926
W. S. Biddle	Aug. 13, 1926
F. T. Hoon	Sept. 21, 1926
B. F. Julian	Dec. 14, 1926
V. W. Tevis	Jan. 10, 1927
H. D. Sterrett	Jan. 25, 1927
F. A. Page	Feb. 15, 1927
W. F. F. Smith	March 26, 1927
William Telfer	April 8, 1927
J. W. Turner	June 25, 1927
H. A. King	Aug. 7, 1927
A. O. Montgomery	Aug. 12, 1927
J. M. Larmore	Aug. 27, 1927
J. M. Baxter	Sept. 16, 1927
J. W. Duncan	Nov. 8, 1927
J. L. Funkhouser	Nov. 29, 1927
A. L. Williams	Feb. 21, 1928

NORTH INDIANA CONFERENCE

Maurice L. Hardingham	May 11, 1924
William Peck	July 5, 1924
Jonah V. Terflinger	July 20, 1924
Titus M. Hill	Aug. 26, 1924
Theodore Frech	Sept. 22, 1924
Schuyler C. Norris	Apr. 26, 1925
Joseph H. James	July 2, 1925
Herbert S. Nickerson	July 3, 1925

Charles E. Disbro ....July 30, 1925
Madison Swadener ....Nov. 16, 1925
John H. French ....Mar. 27, 1926
Thomas J. Johnson ....June 12, 1926
James W. McDaniel ....Aug. 5, 1926
John Phillips ....Oct. 11, 1926
Clarence M. Vawter ....Dec. 17, 1926
Lewis Reeves ....Apr. 16, 1927
Charles H. Brown ....May 21, 1927
Henry Lacy ....May 25, 1927
Robert S. Reed ....Sept. 25, 1927
John M. B. Reeves...Dec. 6, 1927
John S. Cain...Dec. 9, 1927
Edward H. Taylor ....Dec. 28, 1927

NORTHWEST INDIANA CONFERENCE

Henry H. Cannon...July 30, 1924
David Handley ....Oct. 12, 1924
Tiffin F. Drake...Dec. 18, 1924
Henry C. Neal...March 4, 1925
John S. Wright...March 24, 1925
James W. Shell ....Nov. 25, 1925
Charles Jakes ....Jan. 23, 1926
Russell A. Howard...March 6, 1926
Caughey Naylor ....May 20, 1926
James W. Walker...July 6, 1926
William P. McKinsey...March 17, 1927
Benjamin F. Ivey...Feb. 19, 1928

SOUTHERN ILLINOIS CONFERENCE

William C. Macurdy...1924
W. C. Cissna ....Dec. 31, 1924
Milton C. McKown...Jan. 12, 1925
J. W. Britton ....Mar. 30, 1925
D. A. Perrin...July 9, 1925
D. W. Baker...Aug. 24, 1925
Albert Vandaveer ....Mar. 21, 1926
John Wesley Flint...July 4, 1926
Owen H. Clark...Oct. 11, 1926
Nacias B. Cooksey ....Feb. 21, 1927
Samuel Thero ....Apr. 28, 1927
John Wesley Jackson...Mar. 26, 1927
F. M. Van Treese ....Oct. 9, 1927
W. R. Bradley...Dec. 13, 1927
J. E. McCracken...Jan. 13, 1928